52 WAYS

to care for your pastor

Fun, creative, love-in-action ideas to
bless the socks off your pastoral team for
an entire year!

LESLIE EICHLER

Contents

Dedicated to my husband, best friend, and spiritual example of how to shine for Jesus in a dark and fallen world:

Thank you, Ken, for teaching me to default to grace and mercy. Thank you for your love, your belief, and your encouragement.

You were the kindest person I'd ever met when you were my College/Career Pastor all of those years ago. Thirty-eight+ years later you remain the kindest person I've ever known. I'm so glad I asked you out!

Introduction

"And now, friends, we ask you to honor those leaders who work so hard for you, who have been given the responsibility of urging and guiding you along in your obedience. Overwhelm them with appreciation and love." 1 Thessalonians 5:12-13 (The Message)

In the Fall of 2014 I was asked to write a series of articles titled, *52 Ways to Care for Your Pastor*, to be posted as blogs for **Standing Stone Ministry** and to be sent out as weekly emails. Over the course of that year many people asked to receive copies of those posts in order to share them with their friends and members of their churches. This book is a compilation of all *52 Ways* to correspond with one calendar year.

But, who or what is Standing Stone Ministry, you ask? Standing Stone Ministry is a ministry to and for ministry leaders, specifically to *Shepherd Shepherds*. SSM exists to bring love, encouragement, hope, energy, and fun back into the lives of those that serve in our churches. Whether they serve church leadership by hosting a ministry couple during a **one-on-one weeklong retreat**, through a mentoring relationship with a **Standing Stone Shepherd**, or by encouraging pastors' wives through **Ministry Wives Rock** Facebook page for pastors' wives, Standing Stone Ministry's focus is on keeping our shepherds healthy and vitalized in order to best serve the flocks that the Lord has entrusted to them. Obviously I'm pretty passionate about the work of Standing Stone since my husband and I have been with Standing Stone since 2011.

My hope is that as you read each weekly suggestion you will be inspired to apply some of these ideas at your own church and bless and care for your pastor(s). Please don't feel obligated or pressured to carry out *every single suggestion every single week*. That would be too time consuming, too expensive, and let's be honest, too creepy. You want to cause your pastor to feel loved and appreciated not stalked!

And, it's not just the lead pastor that we want to bless. I hope you will apply some of these suggestions to others on staff in a pastoral capacity. Everyone serving in a pastoral/leadership role in the church needs affirmation because, unfortunately, the opposite is actually more common. It's a shame.

I certainly don't want to forget the unsung heroes of the church - ministry wives! I have suggestions for blessing them, as well as the pastor's children. Living life in a fishbowl for all to see and judge is tough. Having healthy and happy spouses and children is an important component to having healthy and happy shepherds!

I look forward to reader comments on how you cared for your pastor or, if you are a pastor, how you felt loved and cared for by members of your congregation. Any comments can be directed to Leslie.e@standingstoneministry.org.

Are you ready to begin a fun journey over the next 52 weeks? Let's go!

Soli De Gloria, *Leslie*

Pray

For this reason, ever since I heard about your faith in the Lord Jesus and your love for all God's people, I have not stopped giving thanks for you, remembering you in my prayers. I keep asking that the God of our Lord Jesus Christ, the glorious Father, may give you the Spirit of wisdom and revelation, so that you may know him better. Ephesians 1:15-17

Can you imagine how the church at Ephesus felt when reading the above words? Paul, the apostle of Jesus Christ by the will of God, was praying for them. Not only was he praying, but he was specifically praying for wisdom and revelation so that the church would know God better. Who wouldn't be encouraged by that?!?!?

Can you imagine how your pastor will feel when you tell him* that you are diligently praying for him?

Can you imagine how he would feel if several people told him the same thing? In the same week? Through spoken words, emails, and cards?

One way, and in my opinion, the most important way to care for your pastor is to **pray**. That's why I'm starting this book with prayer. Pray for your pastor. Pray that God would fill your pastor with wisdom and revelation. Pray that your pastor would hear the voice of God clearly. Pray that your pastor would get to know Christ even better.

However, by *telling* your pastor that you are praying for him you are going one step further; you are making a commitment. You are committing yourself to doing the actual work of prayer intercession and spiritual warfare. Because, the truth is, we are in a war.

For our struggle is not against flesh and blood, but against the rulers, against the authorities, against the powers of this dark world and against the spiritual forces of evil in the heavenly realms.
Ephesians 6:12

Your pastor is on the front lines of this war. He is probably battle weary and battle scarred. He could use the encouragement of knowing that he is not fighting alone. Think of Aaron and Joshua holding up Moses' arms.

Once you **tell** your pastor you are praying for him, you have to **actually pray**! How do you do that on a consistent basis? Glad you asked; I have some suggestions for you.

- Set a timer on your smart phone. We do it all the time to remind us of important appointments. What is more important than an appointment with God to talk about your pastor(s)?

- Write his name on a sticky note and place it on the steering wheel of your car. When you are on your morning commute you can turn off the radio for five minutes and pray.

- Write his name on a piece of paper and place it in a spot that you frequent often; the coffee maker, refrigerator, bathroom mirror, TV remote control. You get it. The point is to be creative and come up with a way to consistently and regularly pray for your pastor(s).

Satan doesn't want us to pray for our pastors, or anyone else for that matter, so expect some resistance. Expect to fall asleep quickly if you intend to pray the last thing at night. Expect the phone to ring the second you sit down to pray. Be prepared to push through the distractions and then.........simply pray!

Pray for wisdom.
Pray for God's peace for him and his family.
Pray for strength.
Pray for encouragement.
Pray for health.
Pray for inspiration.
Pray for a closer walk and for time to spend *on his own* in prayer and the word. You'd be surprised at how many pastors struggle with their own personal devotions.

Pray. Daily. Diligently. Thoughtfully.

And every now and then drop your pastor a note reminding him that he is loved and that you continue to pray for him.

Every now and then shake his hand on the way out of church and tell him that you pray for him every morning at 7 am (or whenever).

Every now and then shoot off an email with an encouraging scripture with the reminder that you are holding up his arms in prayer.

To reiterate; **the #1 way to care for your pastor(s) is to pray.**

*See disclaimer before the Introduction

Week of January 8 through14

Coffee House or Restaurant Gift Card

Some weeks, like this one, will be easy. A gift card can be picked up almost anywhere and can be gifted to your pastor anytime. I wanted to start you off with something simple. Other weeks will take some extra care and advanced planning. I don't want to scare you away before you've barely begun.

So, why the coffee house or restaurant gift card? Is it because most pastors would benefit from a direct intravenous line of caffeine and lemon bars to make it through the day? Nope. Most pastors probably could dial it back a cup or two and they *definitely* don't need more calorie-laden sweets. The **coffee house/restaurant gift card is for others** because, quite often, a pastor will meet people in a safe, public venue such as a coffee house for counseling or mentoring purposes.

Some people find it uncomfortable to meet with the pastor in his office at church. There could be many reasons for this, but having the option of meeting at a local coffee house or restaurant is an easy way for your pastor to minister to others. Also, just **the act of buying the other person a cup of coffee or tea helps set the tone for the entire meeting**. A gift card helps defray the cost to the pastor, which can add up quite quickly.

To be fully honest though, the gift card isn't just for ministering to others. Your pastor might just enjoy a mocha chip macchiato with extra whip now and then after a hard day in the trenches. Nothin' wrong with that.

So what do you think? The next time you're in line for your daily fix of java or soup and sandwich combo, will you consider grabbing a gift card to pass along to your pastor? It will be appreciated!

Week of January 15 through 21

"Adopt" one or more of his* children as someone you pray for, encourage, and support regularly

As a parent I love the idea of someone *adopting* one, or all, of my children in order to pray for them on a regular basis. I love the idea of others coming alongside my children to encourage them in life and in faith. I love the idea of a person or persons supporting my child emotionally, spiritually, and in some instances financially. I'm still grateful to those sweet saints that bought magazine subscriptions and frozen cookie dough so my kids could attend church camp or cheered alongside us at innumerable high school basketball games.

In some cultures and/or denominations godparents are carefully chosen at the child's birth. These godparents nurture the child and take on a very important role during the child's life; the most important being to encourage the child in his/her spiritual walk. In the Methodist church, for instance, during the infant's baptism the godparents will be asked this question, "Will you keep this child in your care and prayers so that he/she may grow in the love of God?" The godparents answer, "I will." It is a very carefully thought out and important undertaking.

What an honor and privilege to be able to provide additional love, care, and nurturing and to be able to speak truth into the lives of little ones and not-so-little ones.

Want to hear some good news? You don't have to be a formal godparent to encourage your pastor's children. You can begin at any time.

Life as a pastor's kid (PK) has lots of perks and pitfalls. Yes, the kids get to share in the fun stuff with their parents, but they are oftentimes criticized and held to a higher standard than other children their same ages. It can be a difficult and confusing journey for a child or teen.

Church members who pray for their pastor's kids, take the time to speak to the children about subjects that interest *the children*, remember their birthdays or special occasions with a card or note, and who include them in activities with their own children and families are operating in that godparent role, without the fancy labels.

My children were fortunate to have a few special adults in their lives as they were growing up. One particular man, Uncle Don (not to be confused with Uncle *Uncle* Don, their dad's brother), was as close to a godfather as they will ever have. He was there at their births. He attended birthday parties, sporting events, graduations, and weddings. He searched the mall for patent leather *Mary Janes* for a 3-year-old. He took a troubled teen out for coffee to speak hard truths into her life (he'd earned that right over the years). He taught one or possibly two of them to drive a manual transmission. He even sat through an agonizing night (for him) of Hagen Das ice cream and three hours of watching *The*

Sound of Music! Why? Because he was committed to helping our children grow in the love and strength of the Lord. My children were, and still are, very fortunate to have such a wonderful person in their lives. We didn't ask Uncle Don to be that person, he volunteered.

You can make a difference in the lives of your PK's. You can pray effectual, fervent prayers over your PK's, even if you don't know them personally. You can send notes and cards. You can acknowledge them as special, unique people, not miniature replicas of their parents. You can offer grace and mercy when they act like the children that they are. And, you can remind others who may be critical or judgmental of the importance of stepping up and supporting these precious, vulnerable ones through prayer, love, and lots of grace. Lots and lots of grace.

I think I just heard all of the PK's the world over shout, "AMEN!"

*See disclaimer

Week of January 22 through 28

Acknowledge birthdays and anniversaries

Here's another easy one, folks. What do you say we find out our pastor(s)' birthday and anniversary dates and overwhelm him/her/them with cards?

Have you ever seen the movie *Miracle on 34th Street*? There is a scene at the end when the U.S. Postal Service delivers bags and bags of mail addressed to Santa Claus to the courtroom where Kris Kringle is on trial. Got that picture in your head? Wouldn't it be fun to reenact a scene like that in your pastor's office? Can you imagine how fun it would be to overwhelm the birthday boy or girl with tons of cards and well wishes?

How about balloons? I know of one pastor that arrived at his office on his birthday to be greeted with a room packed full of helium balloons. The staff had fun with those balloons all day long.

I can think of lots of other ways to acknowledge your pastor's birthday and/or anniversary. All are fun. All speak of love and care, respect and encouragement. Some are just plain crazy, some more conservative. No matter.

Do you think your church could pull off a birthday or anniversary surprise? It sure would be fun to try.

My challenge, if you'll take it, is to find out the birth dates and anniversary dates of each member of your pastoral team and do something fun and out of the box as a way to acknowledge these important milestones. It will be a lot of fun for you and your congregation as you work together to pull off a big surprise.

Ever thought about taking 500 ping pong balls signed by each member of the congregation and, well, you get the idea...

Oh, come on! You know you want to!

Week of January 29 through February 4

Support your church financially

When I first met my husband he was a full time College/Career pastor making $400 a month. By the time we'd gotten engaged he was making $600 a month. Just before we got married he got a raise and was making $800 a month. Thus was my introduction to life as a pastor's wife.

Fast forward 10 years. We'd just planted a new church without any financial support from a denominational or church planting organization. In order to pay the rent and utilities for our house, make a tiny car payment, and put food on the table my husband worked three part-time jobs. The church was barely bringing in enough each month to cover the rent and utilities on our church space so taking a salary was out of the question. I worked at a local Christian school in order for our three children to get a good education, have family medical insurance, and to contribute toward our financial needs.

As the church grew, so did my husband's responsibilities. He finally was able to take a small salary and quit two of his part-time jobs. He still moonlighted as an IT guy for several local businesses for pay and for barter. When enough tithes came in, and our church bills were paid, my husband got a paycheck. Many, many weeks he took no salary or a reduced salary. This was the pattern of our lives for several years. Our experience in ministry during those lean years is not unique. I've heard from many pastors of small-to-medium sized churches facing the same struggles today. When money doesn't come in bills are juggled, staff isn't paid, and life in ministry is tough. Very tough.

When my husband was hired at a mega-church we discovered that financial struggles didn't end, in fact, they were magnified. Giant churches have giant programs with large staffs to meet the needs of the thousands of attendees. One of my husband's duties as a pastor on the Executive Team was to make sure the departments under his area of responsibility stayed within their respective budgets. When tithes were down and times got lean he had to make the hard decisions and cut staff and programs. All were unpopular decisions made necessary by financial shortfalls.

Why do I share this with you? Because **we can care for our pastor(s) by supporting our churches financially**. When money (tithes and offerings) come in, our churches can carry on the daily duties of serving us, our families, our communities, and the world. The size of the congregation doesn't matter. The church depends on its people to cover all of the expenses of rent or mortgage payments, the utility bills to keep us warm in the winter and cool in the summer, and salaries for the pastoral team and support staff. That's reality!

Supporting our church financially isn't just about paying the bills; it is to bless us as well. When we support our churches we are supporting all of the ways that they reach into our communities. It isn't easy to physically minister to the soul needs of a 3-year-old, a homeless vet, a recovering alcoholic, and a refugee on the other side of the world, but through our financial support our church is doing all of those things on our behalf and more! **We become part of the larger community of the family of God.**

Also, just so you know, worries over finances, budgets, layoffs and hiring freezes are a difficult reality for most pastors and are a large contributing factor towards stress and, sadly, burnout. *"Just trust the Lord, He will provide."* some might say. Okaaaaaaay. However, the Lord, for some crazy reason, likes to work through His people to accomplish His will on the earth. One of those ways is through financially giving to the work of the church. In other words, we are to take **some of God's money** and give it to the church, to other organizations where the Lord leads, and keep some for ourselves, **because it pleases God!** But don't just take my word for it. Here's what the Apostle Paul had to say about giving:

> *"Let everyone give as his heart tells him, neither grudgingly nor under compulsion, for God loves the man who gives cheerfully. After all, God can give you everything that you need, so that **you may always have sufficient both for yourselves and for giving away to other people.** As the scripture says: 'He has dispersed abroad, he has given to the poor; his righteousness remains forever'."* 2 Corinthians 9:7-9

I think that pretty much sums it up, don't you?

Take your pastor and his* family off the pedestal. They are human, just like you

When you think about your pastor and his/her family, do images of the perfect television family come to mind? Do you imagine each morning begins with joyful praise and family devotions before mom serves up a nutritious breakfast around the farm-style table? The perfectly groomed kids then happily pile into the minivan carrying their lunches (GMO-free, of course) and backpacks neatly filled with completed homework assignments. Dad drives off in his own car after kissing each child on the cheek and saying a prayer over them.

Not likely.

Now imagine your crazy mornings. Imagine conversations around your table. Imagine how you feel when you've had a busy week with few nights home before the kids are in bed. Imagine days when the laundry is piled up to the ceiling, the washing machine is broken, and Bank of America just let you know your account is overdrawn.

Yeah, the pastor's family is more like that. Truth.

One of the best ways to bless your pastor and his/her family is to take them off the pedestal. They are human. He may have differing political views. She may post something on Facebook that is funny to her, but offensive to you. He may have made the tragic mistake of ordering the garlic lovers pizza before prayer meeting. She may be unaware that the baby spit down her back and the toddler wiped his nose on her sleeve. Their kids are not role models, they're just kids.

Don't get me wrong, answering the call to ministry is a serious endeavor and there is every expectation of leading as an example. There is every expectation of integrity, honesty, godly character, and self-control. Ministry couples, however, aren't the only ones expected to live lives worthy of the name of Christ. There is no imaginary line where ministry families live on one side and laymen live on the other. Sorry to break the news to you.

Your pastor will inspire you, challenge you, and occasionally offend you. That's reality. Your pastor's spouse may meet all of your expectations or none of them. If the latter is true, then you may have unrealistic expectations and need to readjust your thinking. Your pastor's kids will be sweet and funny and naughty and nice and rude and naughty (oh, I already said that, sorry, just thinking about my own son). In short, the pastor and his/her family will be just like your family. Regular people just trying their best to love the Lord their God with all their heart, soul, mind, and strength and to love their neighbors (meaning you and me) as themselves. And, let me tell you from experience, that's not always an easy task.

*See disclaimer

Take him* and his wife to lunch

Lunch. The meal between breakfast and dinner. It is usually much cheaper than dinner and eaten more leisurely than breakfast. This is a great time to invite your pastor and his wife (even children) out for a meal in order to get to know them better and as a way to show your appreciation. Because everyone eats, right?

Sunday may or may not be the best day to take your pastor and his wife/family to lunch. Your pastor may be near-comatose by the time church is over, the people are gone, and the church doors are locked. He may need to go directly home, stuff a burrito in his mouth, and hit the hay for an afternoon nap. Depending on the ages of his children (if any), they may also need to get to bed quickly. In that case, lunch after church would definitely not be the blessing you intended it to be, but another event to grind through, even though they would appreciate the sentiment.

How do you know if Sundays are good for an after-church lunch? Simple. Ask. **If Sundays are less than ideal then plan another day of the week**. Sometimes midweek lunch dates are a welcome change of pace and quite a treat, especially if the kids are in school and the pastor's wife can enjoy adult conversation uninterrupted by little ones.

Here are a few tips regarding lunch:

Including your pastor's wife in the invitation speaks volumes to her. Quite often she feels overlooked and unappreciated for her contribution to the church. If she has small children or works outside of the home give her plenty of options and time to make arrangements. Spur of the moment is great, *if it works*, but can leave a PW (pastor's wife) feeling sad and resentful if she is constantly left out of invitations due of other obligations. Work around her schedule!

Consider their dietary needs before issuing the invitation. If all you can afford is Taco Bell and he is on a restricted low salt/low fat diet then it could be rather awkward. Perhaps plan a midafternoon get together at a local coffee house instead.

If you ask, and they decline due to other obligations, don't get your feelings hurt! Just make a date for another time that works for all parties involved.

Don't be afraid to issue an invitation. Don't assume your pastor is busy. Don't assume they have more invitations than they can handle. Don't assume. Period. Your pastor and his wife are humans who enjoy community with others! So ask already!

*See disclaimer

Week of February 19 through 25

Send him* and his family a greeting card with a message of appreciation and encouragement

I don't know about you, but getting a card in the mail with a personal handwritten note means more to me than a quick email message or e-card. Why? Probably because of the time and effort involved. I know that the person sending the card had to take the time to (1) go to the store and search out the perfect card, (2) purchase the card with money, (3) take the time to write a thoughtful message in *legible handwriting* (as a former school teacher that's a BIG deal to me!) and then (4) address the card, pop on a stamp, and actually get the card into the mailbox.

Effort + thoughtfulness + handwritten words of appreciation and encouragement = feelings of love and care. Warm fuzzies. Don't you like warm fuzzies yourself? Your pastor *and* his wife do too.

This isn't a difficult way to show the leaders of your church that you care about them, but it does take more effort than sitting down at your computer or with your smart phone and punching a few letters on a keypad. A small difference in some ways, yet a huge difference in other ways. Your pastor will feel the love.

Don't know your pastor's home address because you are part of a mega church and your pastor's personal information is kept private for obvious safety reasons? No problem, mail the card to the church in care of Pastor and Mrs. _____. He'll get it. Hopefully he'll remember to take it home to show his wife!

Are you part of a small congregation and know exactly where your pastor lives? Save yourself a postage stamp and drop the card by the house one day with a plate of cookies or a tray of cupcakes. You don't need to linger, just pass the plate (pun intended) and the card to whoever opens the door. Your name will be praised at the gates of the city. I guarantee!

So get thee to the nearest card store and commence the blessings of the written word.

*See disclaimer in Intro

Send them on a Standing Stone retreat

Now that the holidays are over many of us are making plans for summer vacations and weekends away. During these cold months we dream of somewhere, *anywhere*, warm and tropical. This is a great time to also make plans for the ministry couples in your church to attend a Standing Stone retreat.

A Standing Stone retreat consists of one ministry couple spending a week (yep, you read that correctly) with one Retreat Shepherd couple. During the course of the week there is much discussion about ministry, marriage, and building margin into our daily lives. There is also food (lots and lots), fun, and fellowship. Relationships are forged that will last a lifetime. While a ministry couple might initially be reluctant to go away with strangers, by the end of the week they are very glad that they did. Their marriages are strengthened, their bodies and spirits have been refreshed, and they feel encouraged and eager to jump back into their ministries at home. Of course it doesn't hurt that many of our host homes are in warm and tropical locations.

Here are a few quotes directly from ministry couples that have attended a Standing Stone retreat:

"In one week we have been able to experience so much fun, yet also be nurtured in ways we both desperately needed.

Thank you for caring for us so sincerely and for making us feel cherished and valuable."

"God wanted to show His love, kindness, wisdom, and goodness to us at this critical point in our lives. We needed a place and space to take a breath, be in awe, lick some wounds, and find some rest."

"For the first time my wife was able to connect with someone who really understands the daily stress of the expectations our congregation puts on her and our family."

We had one pastor and his wife attend a retreat at the beginning of a three month sabbatical. They were close to leaving the ministry entirely and desperately needed a break. They found that and so much more during their weeklong retreat. A few years after attending his own retreat, that pastor and his church board made it possible for each ministry couple in their large church to attend a Standing Stone retreat.

Attending a Standing Stone retreat is not a vacation, though there is plenty of time for fun in the sun. Rather, attending a retreat is a preventative measure. Instead of waiting until your pastor or spouse is so frustrated, overwhelmed, discouraged, burnt out, and ready to walk away from ministry, take the initiative now to send your pastor and his/her spouse on a retreat. Talk with your church board members and make plans for later in the year. You've got the time, now make something happen. A healthy shepherd helps create healthy congregations. Healthy congregations have lasting impacts on their communities and the world.

Want more information? Contact Standing Stone Ministry directly at www.standingstoneministry.org and partner with Standing Stone to care for your ministry leaders!

Week of March 5 through 11

Volunteer to minister to the homebound or make hospital visits

Volunteering is a beautiful thing. Not only are you meeting a need in the church, but you experience personal fulfillment when you volunteer to serve others.

My husband and I served at a church with the strongest volunteer force I'd ever seen, which was good since the church had more than 5,000 people attend on any given weekend. The lead pastor was a wise man and encouraged the church members on a weekly basis to (1) serve in their area of passion and (2) recruit others to do the same. A simple, yet brilliant formula.

Finding our area of passion is important. If I am being constantly reminded, cajoled, or pushed to show up to serve in a particular ministry in the church, then I probably don't feel very passionate about that area of ministry. However, if I find myself looking forward to the next event, class, or meeting because I can't wait to roll up my sleeves and jump in, then I've probably found an area of passion. Once I've discovered my area of passion it is human nature to want to tell others and to invite them to join me. That's how strong volunteer teams are formed. However, they don't form themselves organically. It will take leadership to encourage people to begin the process of finding their area of passion in which to serve.

What's your area of passion? What floats your boat? Don't know? Try several ministry opportunities to find the one that suits you best.

One area of ministry that is often neglected is that of visiting people who are homebound or hospitalized. It certainly isn't a very glamorous ministry and people won't know who you are because you won't get any face time in front of the congregation. Don't care about accolades and fanfare? Good, you're already ahead of the game. Are you a good listener? Do you enjoy praying with people? Does your heart fill with compassion for the sick and hurting? Your church might have a volunteer program to visit the sick or those who cannot get around well due to physical limitations. Some training may be involved, but the biggest requirement is the heart to love others and to give the gift of your time. Some churches have lay-leaders that bring communion to shut-ins and those in nursing homes and assisted living facilities. Does that interest you?

When you find your area of passion do yourself, your church, your pastor, and your community a favor and spend some of your precious time volunteering. **Don't allow busyness or lack of time to rob you of the blessing of serving others.** In serving others you are serving your pastor(s) and ultimately serving the Lord through His people. Then, take that next step and recruit others to join you. Share your passion. I guarantee your pastor will be thrilled. I'll say it again, volunteering is a beautiful thing. **Be beautiful.**

Week of March 12 through 18

Drop off goodies at the church office for the staff to enjoy

Lest we forget about all of the others that serve us through our local church, we are going to focus on the church staff, which means EVERYONE ELSE that plays a role in regular church life. I don't want to create a list because I'd invariably forget an important department and ruffle feathers. By EVERYONE ELSE I mean everyone other than the lead pastor, although he/she, too, can share in the bounty of generosity this post will inspire.

Most churches have a *fat counter*, i.e., the place where all goodies donated to the church are stored for 0.7 seconds before the hallways are full of people pushing and shoving to get to the above mentioned goodies. We had such a *fat counter* (I don't know how the name came about, that's just what it was called) at a former church and almost daily people dropped off things much to our collective gastric delight. Was there an extra half sheet cake from a wedding reception? How about a tray of muffins from the Ladies' Tea? Did someone have a bag of grandma's homemade oatmeal cookies that the kids didn't like because raisins are not the same as chocolate chips? No problem, give it to the church! We were happy to take pretty much anything and everything, hence the name, Fat Counter. We loved it! We appreciated it! We looked forward to having a treat (or several) each day. We even liked the healthy stuff!

So, if you'd like to bless your church staff, including any volunteers hanging around, then drop by your church with your offering of goodies. They don't have to be store bought because leftovers are equally appreciated. Just be sure and give the offering to the church receptionist or Administrative Assistant to pass out in a judicious manner because those Youth Ministers have a nose for the good stuff like a bloodhound on the trail of wild boar.

Week of March 19 through 25

Choose To Forgive

Easter season is upon us. Depending on the calendar year we will soon be celebrating the death and resurrection of our Savior or we have recently taken part in Easter festivities. One of the most sacred days of Easter is Good Friday; the day we humbly and gratefully remember the sacrifice of Jesus Christ on the cross. Why did Jesus die? The shedding of blood was necessary for the forgiveness of sin. Jesus paid the ultimate price so that you and I could be forgiven.

Matthew 18:21-22 gives us the account of Peter asking Jesus how many times he must forgive someone who sins against him. I'm sure Peter felt pretty magnanimous when he suggested seven times. However, Jesus responded with a surprising figure – seventy times seven. Say what? I'm supposed to forgive someone 490 times? Really? Yes. *Really*.

Have you ever been offended by something your pastor said? Have you ever been hurt, disappointed, angered, or frustrated by a person or persons related to your church or a church activity?

One of the best ways to care for your pastor is to forgive. Forgive your pastor. Forgive members of the congregation. Forgive *the church* in general. There is no greater blessing in a pastor's life than to have a church full of healthy people who are quick to forgive and who extend grace and mercy to others.

Unforgiveness hinders our ability to enter into fellowship with other believers. I know of an old gentleman who showed up at his church week after week, year after year. He would slip into the same pew at the back of the church just as the song service ended and slip out just before the final prayer. He was not there to support the church though. He was there to protest. He was angry with certain decisions that had been made years earlier. It did not involve moral failure or misappropriation of funds. Rather, it had to do with *the decor in the church foyer* (I am not making this up). To my knowledge he has not been able to get past the hurt and unforgiveness and is still registering his protests to this day.

Unforgiveness can turn us into bitter, angry people. Several years ago I was invited to join a mid-week Bible study in the home of a woman from a church other than my own. The leader of the group had an issue with their pastor's wife and rather than refer to her by name called her "that woman". Her contempt was clearly evident. Needless to say I did not return.

Unforgiveness eats away at the very core of our being. It makes us sick. It infects others. It is a cancer. We know this, yet, it isn't always easy to forgive. Let me rephrase that. It isn't always easy to *feel* forgiveness. But forgiveness, like love, is a choice. The feelings may not immediately follow the action and that's okay. I've often rephrased Mark 9:24 and prayed, *"Lord, I forgive. Now help me feel forgiveness."* It is a process. I've found in due time the feelings come and with them comes a lightening of my heart and spirit. Unforgiveness is a heavy weight to carry around.

Whether this week we observe Good Friday or not; today is a good day to lay any *past hurt or heavy burden of unforgiveness* at the foot of the cross and in its place receive peace. Peace that only He can give.

Week of March 26 through April 4

Have a quarterly or semi-annual church "refresh" day

Whether you attend a very large church or a very small church it is a fact that church buildings get dirty, need repairs, and the landscaping needs constant attention. Larger churches have budgets (some very large) for a team of custodians that spend their days cleaning, repairing, painting, trimming, and mowing. Smaller churches often rely on one person to keep up with things or they recruit volunteers who take turns cleaning the rooms, carpets, and restrooms on a weekly basis. When my husband and I had a church of about 200+ people we used volunteers to keep things clean, because we simply didn't have any extra dollars in our budget to hire cleaners. It was a great system when it worked; i.e., when the volunteers actually showed up! There were many, many, *many* times that I got a call on a Sunday morning asking if the kids and I could come early and do some cleaning since those scheduled to come in the day before had forgotten. To be fair, no one deliberately failed to show up for their appointed cleaning day, they simply forgot. The end result, either way, was the pastor and his family had to scramble to tidy things up before people arrived.

Other than the usual daily or weekly cleaning (emptying trashcans, moping, dusting, vacuuming) it is necessary to do deep cleaning at least four times a year. Does your church have a budget for that? Could your classrooms do with a bit of touching up with paint? Does your carpet need shampooing? Do you have cobwebs in hard to reach places? Are the light fixtures full of dirt and dust?

What about the church grounds? Does your church hire professionals to mow the lawn, trim the trees, and plant flowers and shrubs seasonally?

Would it seem too radical of an idea if I proposed that church members volunteer their time and skills four times a year or, at the very least, twice a year to spruce things up inside and out? Even if your church has a giant budget to do these things wouldn't it be great if a portion of that money could go into a benevolence fund or missions fund? A few times a year church members could take care of some of the upkeep on a *Church Refresh Day* rather than hiring professional landscapers, painters, or carpet cleaners.

I've volunteered at several church cleanup or refresh days over the years. They were a lot of fun! We all worked hard scrubbing and making needed repairs and loved every minute of it. Why? Because we were building community. We were serving the church body by caring for the church buildings and grounds. We were getting to know one another on a different and deeper level by working side by side. Stories flowed, laughter ensued, friendships were made, and the body of Christ grew stronger.

Take a look around your church buildings and grounds this Sunday. Do you see areas that could use a little fixing up? Why not volunteer to organize a church refresh day this Spring? Your pastor would love it as it would lighten his/her load and allow him/her to check off one more item on the church **To Do** list. You'll enjoy yourself, as will all those who volunteer their time and skills, plus you'll be making your church a more welcoming place. Scuffed walls, cobwebby corners, and chocolate chip-like stained carpets don't make the best first impression on visitors. *You* can make a definite difference and be a huge blessing to your ministry leaders.

Offer to fill up your pastor's gas tank

This week's way to care for your pastor seems pretty self-explanatory, doesn't it? Your pastor has a car. Your pastor's car runs on gasoline (or diesel). Your pastor needs to fill up the gas tank regularly. Therefore, offering to fill up the gas tank with fuel is a very useful and practical way to show that you care.

I could just stop there. But I won't.

First, let me define **who** I mean by *pastor*. I mean anyone in a pastoral leadership role in your church; not just the person up front each week. You know that young man (who is married with a young child) that works with the high school and junior high kids? Did you know that he consistently picks up and drops off kids that are too young to drive and that he often meets students under his care at various locations around town in order to encourage and mentor them? That uses up quite a bit of gasoline. How about the Children's Pastor that had to dash out a gazillion times to pick up items needed for the Christmas program or Vacation Bible School? Did you think about the Single's Pastor that had a 3-hour road trip to meet up for a weekend event? I could go on.........but you get the idea.

I want to expand your thinking when I discuss Leader Care. I want to encourage you to care for *all of your church leadership* in practical ways that say **I care about you**.

So, practically speaking, cash, a gift card, or one-time credit card (purchased at most grocery stores) can be slipped into an envelope and handed to the pastor (of your choice) with an explanation of intent and a note of thanks. Easy enough, right? Especially if he/she doesn't know you well enough to hand you the keys to the car!

As with any of these **52 Ways to Care for Your Pastor** you are under no obligation. No arm twisting. No guilt. My purpose is to simply help everyone *think outside of the box* when it comes to ways to encourage and support those who spend their lives trying to encourage and support us and our families.

Week of April 9 through 15

Use social media to give a thumbs up

I would certainly be remiss if I didn't remind everyone that giving a shout out or a thumbs up to your pastor on social media is a quick and very easy way of affirming and appreciating the job that he/she is doing. Most of us have Facebook accounts. Many have Twitter, Instagram, and/or LinkedIn accounts. It would be the work of a couple of seconds to make a post or send a hashtag message telling the world that you appreciate your pastor(s), your church, or a particular message.

I just checked my Facebook newsfeed; I watched a video with cute baby goats, saw that someone was eating lunch (using a selfie stick I might add), received an invitation to join a squat challenge (don't ask), read six or seven *sort of* funny memes, two friends encouraged me to pray, and one friend just checked into Starbucks. I know that my feed is constantly updated, but so far no one has mentioned that they appreciated last weekend's church service or thanked their worship leader for leading them into the presence of the Lord. I'm not being judgmental or preachy here; I'm just saying that there is plenty of room on social media to care for your pastor by way of a post, tweet, or whatever else your social site of choice calls an update.

It is probably very likely that your pastor is on Facebook. Most churches have a Facebook page, why not start there? If you wrote a post thanking your pastor for the hard work that he/she does every day to serve your church, I'll bet that several of your friends would **like** the post or would add a comment. If you added your pastor's name or your church's name to the post, your pastor will be notified that he/she was mentioned. I know your pastor will enjoy reading all of the nice things people will say. I certainly enjoy it when people like something I post or say kind words when I change my profile picture. I call them cyber-hugs.

So, #whatdoyousay? Can you give your pastor a shout out, thumbs up, or cyber-hug today?

#Sureyoucan.

#Itiseasy.

#Everybodylovestofeelappreciated!

If something touched your heart during the message make an encouraging comment expressing specifically how it touched you

There are two words that express a universal human longing. I don't care who you are, where you live, your age, your socioeconomic background, your religion, or your gender. We're all the same, end of story, period, infinity.

Those two words are **affirmation** and **appreciation**.

We *all* need **positive statements** that give us emotional support or encouragement (affirmation) and to be **recognized as someone of worth** and enjoyed for the good qualities that we possess or for something we have done (appreciation).

All of us. Even your pastor.

How hard would it be for you to stop and tell your pastor what specifically he or she said during the message that especially touched your heart or challenged your thinking? Not hard at all. If the pastor is unavailable or engaged in conversation and you don't want to wait around, send an email to the church office or write a quick note and drop it in the offering box on your way out.

I have a friend that attends a local mega church. Each Sunday, for years, she would write a short note to the pastor to thank him for making a particular point or for sharing a scripture that stirred her thinking or touched her heart. She would sign her name and drop it in the box at the back of the sanctuary. She had never been formally introduced and had no pretentions that he even knew her name. But one Sunday, as she was leaving a local restaurant, she saw the pastor and his family having lunch. She dropped by the table, said a quick hello and thank you, and then introduced herself. He said, *"I know who you are, Maggie, and I have appreciated every single note you've written to me over the years."* My friend was blown away. She had no idea that her simple act of affirming and appreciating the pastor meant so much to him. But it did. She might have been one of thousands that heard his message each week, but, I guarantee you, only a handful ever expressed their appreciation in such a specific way.

On the other hand, I know a young man that labored week after week to prepare thoughtful, inspirational messages during his first pastorate. A sweet old saint stopped him one Sunday morning and said, *"You did a good job this morning, young man. One of these days you'll be a fine preacher!"* I'm sure she meant it as a compliment, but it wasn't received as such. It stung. He didn't feel at all affirmed or appreciated. In fact, 15 years after the fact he still talks about it, though now he laughs.

Affirming and appreciating your pastor can become a habit that spills over to other members of the staff, the church body, your family, your work place, and your community.

Week of April 23 through 29

Know the name of the pastor's spouse and children - greet them by name when you see them

Does it seem strange to you that I would encourage people to learn their pastor's spouse's name? You'd expect everyone would know the name of the pastor's wife/husband, wouldn't you? Yet, in larger churches or in the case of a pastor other than the lead or preaching pastor it is quite possible that a large percentage of the congregation wouldn't know the name of the pastor's spouse. The same is true for the pastor's kids.

In my previous life, I've been introduced as Mrs. Pastor Ken or "the pastor's wife" because the person making the introductions didn't know my name. Whenever that happened we joked about it and I made sure to let them know my real name, but it was awkward. I imagine this scenario happens quite frequently in the case of the pastor's children; I know it happened to my own kids.

So what do we do if we don't know who is married to the administrative pastor, the youth pastor, the children's pastor, or the worship leader? Ask someone in the know to point out the spouse and then make a mental note to remember the name and the face. Better yet, walk over and introduce yourself to the spouse and strike up a conversation. I guarantee you'll remember her/him in the future and will be able to greet her/him by name. You both will feel good about it. It is good to be recognized for who you are and not just who you've married.

Let's talk about the kids for a moment. It is important to greet the children in an *appropriate* way. A quick, "Hello, Jack" as you're walking down the church hallway is appropriate, especially if you don't really know young Jack. I wouldn't suggest you hunt down the pastor's kids and try to strike up a deep conversation. You'll come across as creepy. Also, if you want to say a word to the pastor and notice that he/she is talking to one of his/her children, be respectful of the child, as well as the pastor, *by waiting patiently for that conversation to end*, acknowledge the child by name, and *then* greet the pastor and have your conversation. I've watched in agony as my own children were ignored or interrupted because someone wanted a word with their father. I'm sure no disrespect was intended, but my kids felt disrespected nonetheless.

I hope you've found this little tip helpful. I wouldn't be surprised if the majority of readers don't know the name of the worship leader's wife or the children's pastor's husband. I've just realized that I've got some homework to do of my own. Do you?

Don't forget to show appreciation to the other pastors on staff (executive, worship, youth, etc.) and heads of ministry

This is now week 18 of our **52 Ways to Care.** By now, if you've been reading in chronological order, you've been encouraged to express your thanks to your pastor, buy him gift cards for coffee and such, take him and his wife to lunch, and even send them away on a marriage retreat. Hopefully you've been able to act on a couple of suggestions and have one or two ideas for the future tucked away in your mind. Your pastor is probably feelin' the love.

But, before I go any further, I'd be remiss if I didn't remind you to also include other pastors on staff and heads of ministry to the list. I'm sure you already knew these others were implied, if not expressly mentioned, and have been scheming behind the scenes to bless the socks off of the guys in the media ministry or the director of Women's Ministry. But what about those that work diligently behind the scenes and don't get much face time with the congregation? There are so many busy worker bees on staff in pastoral positions or heads of ministry in the less glamorous areas of ministry that make the wheels go round each week. Please don't forget about them. Every single (well, most) of these ways to show you care can be applied to just about anyone on staff. Spread the love.

Week of May 7 through May 13

Schedule a Sunday to take over the service

This week's suggestion takes some forward planning. It involves giving your pastor or other key ministry leaders a weekend off. In essence, you're kicking them out and telling them to go away for the day or weekend and have a great time. Or sleep in. Their choice.

In order to successfully pull this one off you'll have to have your pastor's cooperation, of course, otherwise it could look like a mini-coup. You don't want your pastor to worry that you're kicking him out of the pulpit. You want to be a blessing, not an additional source of stress!

So, once you've told your pastor your plans to give him/her a day of rest from official pastoral duties, you'll need to find a replacement for the day. I'm sure there are retired pastors in your congregation that would love to get back in the saddle. The college pastor may love a chance at "the big time". Or, the pastor may know of someone that he's wanted to invite to share a word with the congregation. Then, go with it. Pick a future date, make some calls, and give your pastor an unexpected blessing of a Sabbath day – that isn't considered part of his vacation!

Do you want to know why I think it is important to give every member of your pastoral staff an unexpected day off? Because ministry is stressful. Coming up with something meaningful to share week after week takes its toll. Think back to your own high school and college years. Would you have enjoyed writing a paper every single week and then presenting it to the class to be judged on its merit and value? Does it sound like a lot of work and tiring mental gymnastics to find something new and fresh to talk about? Well, that's how your pastor feels. Some run out of ideas and resort to downloading sermons from the internet. It's the truth. I talked to a pastor recently that admitted to using Sermon Central because he had run out of ideas and didn't have the time to develop new material on his own. He, and probably hundreds of pastors across America, all gave the same sermon for Mother's Day because administrative duties and urgent daily needs robbed him of the necessary time to go away with The Father and reflect on His word - not to mention the fact that he was just plain tired.

That's why an unexpected day off here and there can go far in restoring the spring to your pastor's step. However, it's not only the lead or teaching pastor that could use the blessing of a day off. All, yes, ALL of the pastoral staff would benefit from having someone else teach the junior high students on a Sunday morning or take the young marrieds class during the 9:30 am service. You *know* the children's pastor would appreciate a Sunday morning where someone *else* received those early morning calls saying four volunteers aren't available to work the nursery and three-year-old class.

Call it a break. Call it a mental health day. Call it anything you like as long as you call your pastor and begin the process of giving him/her/them a non-vacation weekend off.

May 14 through 20

Treat your pastor's wife to a spa day

As a woman I must confess that I love anything spa related. I love massages, facials, and mani's and pedi's. I think it is the feeling of being pampered – even if it is only for an hour. There is just something luxurious about a good quality spa that is reviving to one's spirit. I don't think I'm alone in that feeling or the spa industry wouldn't be growing so rapidly.

Let's face it, life is stressful. Life as the wife of a ministry leader is doubly stressful because our lives are lived in a fishbowl, as it were. Everyone in the church is aware of who we are. Just because we said "I do" to the man we are somehow elevated above the rest and we are held to a higher degree of scrutiny. The same goes for our kids, for reasons I have yet to understand. It isn't fair, but there it is. It is reality for the majority of ministry wives.

At times, ministry wives are also invisible. It is a paradox, isn't it? On one hand they are highly scrutinized, i.e., what they wear, what they drive, who their friends are, whether they work outside of the home or not, the cleanliness of their homes, or lack thereof, and the list goes on and on. On the other hand they feel invisible because their husbands are recognized for their contributions to the church, but the woman behind the man is ignored. As I shared previously, I was often introduced as Mrs. Pastor Ken or "the pastor's wife" because the person making the introduction didn't know my name!

Have you ever considered how much of a pastor's time is spent at the church, at meetings, making visitations, counseling, and other ministry-related endeavors that keep him away from home many, many evenings? I realize it is the nature of his job, but during all of that time away from home there is usually a woman who is home – alone. If the pastor and his wife have children, then the wife is at home feeding children, supervising homework, overseeing baths, and putting children to bed without the aid of her spouse. Even if she went into the marriage with her eyes wide open and completely aware of all of the ways in which his job would intrude on family time (which, let's face it, NO ONE is completely prepared for life as a PW) it is still difficult.

So here's where a spa day comes in. It isn't mandatory, but it sure is a nice way to tell your pastor's wife that you appreciate her and her contributions to your church. There are so many ways to accomplish this that don't have to break the bank. Here are a few suggestions:

- Gather a group of ladies and invite her for lunch and a pedicure.
- Ask several people to contribute to a group spa day for all of the pastor's wives to enjoy together on a Saturday morning.
- Arrange for a free makeover at the Estee Lauder counter or another counter at a department store and then take her to coffee.

In the event that your pastor's wife doesn't enjoy spa days, then ASK her what she would prefer instead! To spa or not to spa isn't important. Being noticed and appreciated is important.

May 21 through 27

Let the family use your vacation home or timeshare – schedule now before summer begins!

Summer is almost here! Kids will soon be finished with the school year and families are making plans for a vacation trip. Your pastor and his/her family are no exception. Everyone looks forward to the Dog Days of Summer and a little time for R & R.

Do you have a vacation home or a timeshare that will go unused for a week or so during these next few months? Is it possible to offer the use of your vacation home or timeshare to your pastor and his/her family?

I have very happy memories of trips given to my family from a friend/member of our church that worked at a timeshare company. The first time she approached us with a trip to a resort in Mazatlán my husband and I were astonished. We were poor church mice just barely scraping by. We had three kids ranging from elementary school to high school and had never considered the possibility of going away by ourselves (without kids) because we knew we didn't have the finances. However, once we were offered a free stay we somehow figured out a way to pay for our airfare. I cannot tell you how much the trip blessed us, our marriage, and in many ways our ministry. We'd never taken the time away to just relax and play. We came home refreshed and eager to jump back into ministry.

Since then this same precious woman has given us the opportunity to take our kids on a trip to Kauai and to have a place to stay near the army base when our son came home from at 15-month deployment in Iraq – indisputably the happiest day of my life! Her thoughtfulness has blessed my life in ways she will never completely know or understand.

If you are someone fortunate enough to have a second home or timeshare and you know that the house/timeshare will go unused, please consider the thought of allowing your pastor or other ministry couples from your church, or even a local church, the use of your property. Time away to just relax, have fun, play in the sun, and enjoy family is a precious commodity. Your generosity can make that happen.

Week of May 28 through June 3

Meet at his* house on his day off in order to fix things around the place

I hate to burst any bubbles, but that dynamic preaching machine that can effortlessly translate from the original Greek or Hebrew text on a Sunday morning might be all thumbs on a Monday morning when he tries to fix a dripping faucet or leaking toilet. Even if he is a more-than-adequate DIY'er he may have a *Honey Do List* a mile long because he is often called away for various ministry purposes or, probably more honestly, he's just too pooped out on his days off to accomplish many tasks.

If you're a Mr./Ms. Fix It and would love to bless your pastor (AND his wife) then make arrangements to meet at his house on one of his days off and fix some things around the place. Are you an electrician? Ask if he has any need for your services. Are you a painter, plumber, auto mechanic, or all around handyman? Same thing. There are probably several jobs that need doing inside and out.

Even if your pastor loves to tinker around the house you can always ask him if he could use an extra pair of hands. After all, "A problem shared is a problem halved." and "Many hands make the task light." Am I right? He'll appreciate the help and the companionship, especially if the job is a tough one.

Of course I'm assuming you have some skills. Need I elaborate?

This could be a really fun idea if there are a few larger projects that need attention and a (skilled) work crew was assembled to knock out the jobs in short order. You could even add a few great cooks and their culinary contributions to sweeten the pot! Hard work, great food, and fun fellowship. Win-win for everyone.

So what are you waiting for? Snap on your tool belt and make that call!

*See disclaimer

Week of June 4 through 10

Ask for specific prayer needs – then follow up

I've got another easy one for you. You don't have to invite your pastor into your home, buy him dinner, volunteer to clean toilets, or spend a dollar! All I'd like for you to do this week to care for your pastor is to ask him/her **specifically** how YOU can pray for them this week. That's it. Then, go home and ACTUALLY PRAY. Next week check in with your pastor and see how things are going and if there has been any answer to prayer or change in the circumstances.

Pretty easy, huh? Aren't you glad that you don't have much to do? I'll bet you're thinking there must be a catch. In the previous weeks I've asked you to get out of your comfort zone a bit in order to reach out to your pastor and other ministry leaders in your church. Well........you're right. There is a catch.

It isn't enough to simply ASK your pastor how you can pray. If you ask, then you are expected to follow through and actually PRAY. Every day. All week.

The Bible tells us that, *"The effective prayer of a righteous man can accomplish much."* James 5:16 (NASB). The Holman Christian Standard Bible translates the verse as *"The intense prayer of the righteous is very powerful."*
I want my prayers to be very powerful and to accomplish much; I know you do, too. How do we go about it? I believe

that making a commitment to set aside a little time every day, for a week, to pray for your pastor would be a very powerful thing indeed. When we purposefully and intentionally intercede for him/her; lifting up specific needs or circumstances to the Father we can be assured that our God is hearing us and is working all things together for the good (Romans 8:28) on our pastor's behalf.

But how do we remember to pray every day for our pastor if it isn't already a habit? I have a few tricks I use, because I've been guilty of saying, "I'll pray for you" and then promptly forgetting my promise as soon as I walked away.

- Place your watch on the opposite wrist. Every time you check the time you'll be prompted to pray – because you'll be constantly checking both wrists.

- Set a timer on your phone to coincide with a quiet time during your day to stop and pray in earnest.

- Place a sticky note in the middle of your bathroom mirror. Each morning upon arising you'll see the note when you go to brush your teeth or shave and be reminded to stop first and pray, then proceed with your morning ritual.

- Place a sticky note on your computer screen or any place that will give you a mental jolt when you see it in order to prompt you to pray.

Finally, when you're back at church the following Sunday, follow up with your pastor and see how he/she is doing. Tell him/her that you've been specifically praying every day and that you will continue to pray (if there has been no change). Your pastor will be touched and will feel cared for and loved. And, I might add, you'll feel pretty good yourself.

Week of June 11 through 17

Invite the kids on an outing

Just as ministry can take its toll on adults, it can also take its toll on children. When mom (or dad) is blessed by others, the kids are blessed as well. When dad (or mom) is criticized by others, the kids get hurt too. **I often wonder if people give enough thought to how their words and actions affect the pastor's kids.** Kids can suffer from ministry burnout and fatigue just as readily as their parents.

To that end, I'd like to suggest inviting your pastor's children to go on an outing with your family. Some pastoral families live on shoestring budgets and don't have discretionary cash to do extra fun stuff like amusement parks, ballgames, or concerts. Some pastors make a good income and have the extra cash, but they don't always have the extra time. Just because dad is contractually obligated to be at church 48 Sundays a year doesn't mean the kids are as well (translation: yes, they CAN go away with your family for a weekend).

Of course an outing with your family doesn't need to be an expensive one. If your kids enjoy it, the pastor's kids will like it too. A day at the park, a movie, bowling, hiking, bike riding.......you get the idea. I just think it's important for the kids to be included and made to feel special because of who THEY are, not for what their mom or dad does.

Do I need to mention that all of this is predicated on the fact that you or your children already have a relationship with the pastor's kids? Good, I didn't think so.

Week of June 18 through 24

Allow her personal business to remain her personal business

Back in the late 80's my husband was on staff at a 10,000+ member church. The associate pastor's wife had very short, very thin hair. That is until the Sunday she showed up at church with long hair to her waist. Huh? No one had ever heard of hair extensions before. Wanna bet that most people in the church became very familiar with hair extensions soon thereafter? Hair extensions became the hot topic of conversation.

"Do you believe she flew all the way to Chicago to have that done?"
"Well, I want to know who paid for that!"
"Is my tithe money going toward those hair thingies?"
"She must be very vain."
"Obviously she wants everyone to look at her."

I know it is human nature to be curious. When we don't know the answer to a question we tend to speculate. We fill in the blank. The only problem is *we usually fill in the blank with the wrong answer!*

Now let's try that again. This time I'll fill in the blanks with the right answers.

"Do you believe she flew all the way to Chicago to have that done?" **Yes. Big deal. She's a former flight attendant and gets FREE trips – anywhere.**

"Well, I want to know who paid for that!" **Obviously she and her husband paid for it. From their *personal* bank account. They did not steal the offering and sprint off to Chicago.**

Is my tithe money going toward those hair thingies?" **Your tithe money goes towards staff salaries, among other things. What the staff chooses to do with their own personal money is none of your business.**

"She must be very vain." **No. She's just had very fine, short hair her entire life and wondered what it would be like to have a full head of hair, even if it was only temporarily.**

"Obviously she wants everyone to look at her." **See above.**

Besides the wife of the President of the United States, I can't think of an occupation where the wife is under constant surveillance, scrutiny, and (dare I say) *judgment* than a pastor's wife. Can you? Why is that? We notice where she sits in church and with whom. We notice who she talks to and (more importantly) who she *doesn't* talk to. We notice how she's dressed, the cut, style, and color of her hair, and the type of jewelry she wears. We notice what kind of car she drives. If we've ever been invited into her home we notice how she's decorated the house, how clean or cluttered the house is, and whether her kitchen is spotless or dirty – even if we dropped by unannounced!

Just so you know; it's okay to notice. We're all curious to see how other people live. However, when the noticing becomes gossip and speculation, then we've crossed the line. When the noticing causes us to make judgments about our pastor's wife based on no, or very limited, information then we are doing her and ourselves a great disservice.

Can we just agree to allow our pastor's wife to have a personal life? Is it okay for her to make decisions of a personal nature without the approval of the Board, the church body, or the church old biddy? Can we make a pact to shut down gossip and speculation when we hear it?

One of the *very* best ways we can care for our pastor is to care for and protect his wife. 'Nuff said? I thought so.

Week of June 25 through July 1

Offer him* and his wife free sessions with a financial planning consultant to help them budget for college and retirement

News flash! Your pastor didn't go into ministry for the money. And no, your pastor does not get to keep all of the money in the offering plate.

We all have bills. We all need to save for the future. Yet, the reality for many ministry couples is they are too busy just trying to get through this week's round of appointments and next month's obligations to give too much thought to what might happen 20, 30, or 40 years in the future. I know I sure didn't.

A quick Google search lists several studies showing that pastors make significantly less money per year than other professionals with similar educational backgrounds and skill sets. Unless your church has a designated 403b plan (non-profit equivalent of 401k) it is probably a good bet that he or she could use a little help in the retirement planning and/or children's college fund department. Like anyone else just trying to make ends meet, most ministry couples would benefit from a few meetings with a financial planner.

So how do you broach the subject with your pastor without offending him or her? Finances are a very private matter;

you don't want to come across in a way that would suggest any judgment on your part. Here are a few tips for you.

If you are a church board member (and the other members agree) you could simply tell the pastor that you'd like to make a few sessions with a financial planning consultant part of his/her compensation package, if you don't already have an automatic retirement plan (403b) in place (which, sadly is the reality of a majority of churches, especially with smaller congregations).

If you are a member of the congregation and would like to bless your pastor, then *make an offer* to pay for a few sessions. You could explain how you have benefited by having a more formalized plan in place and you'd love to bless him and his family with such a gift. Making an offer is just that – making an offer. There is less risk of having your good intentions misconstrued this way.

Give him/her some seed money (like many grandparents do with savings bonds, etc.) and tell him/her you'd like to contribute to their retirement plan or their children's college fund. That money can be invested in mutual funds, IRA's, or whatever means they choose. You could even walk them through the opening of an account if you are very familiar with this type of thing. Or, direct them to someone who can help (like a *competent* financial consultant).

The bottom line is this, we all know we should be contributing towards our futures - but we don't always follow through. Your pastor (like me and possibly you, too) may just need that extra nudge to get the ball rolling toward a more secure financial future.

Week of July 2 through 8

Take him* golfing

Have you noticed the little asterisk that appears every now and then next to the words *he, his,* or *him,* such as in the above title? It directs you to a disclaimer that says something like - *I realize pastors can be men and women and I'm not trying to be sexist.* I don't assume all pastors are men, even though the title of this particular suggestion mentions taking **him** golfing. You can take **her** golfing too. Really, it's okay with me.

In America we are entering a three, or in some cases, a four-day holiday. People all over the country will take time off of work to celebrate America's Independence Day. Hopefully the weather in your neck of the woods is cooperating and you're enjoying blue skies, white puffy clouds, and bearable temperatures with little-to-no mosquitos. What plans do you have for the weekend? Are you doing anything that can include your pastor and perhaps his family members as well?

Does your pastor enjoy golfing? If the courses in your town aren't overrun with holiday crowds you might want to see if he (or she) has time to slip away for 18 holes, or maybe just 9. Do you have Sea-Doos or another type of water craft? How about an invitation to a day at the lake or river? Does your pastor love to fish? This is a good weekend to try out the new rod and reel.

Is your pastor busy? Out of town? Overrun with other invitations? That's okay. Make your offer and set up another possible date down the road. I promise he/she would love another opportunity to get in some play time during the long, hot days of summer. I speak from personal experience here.

Don't forget his/her family!! The kids would enjoy a day at the beach, lake, river, or pool. Camping for a few days during the week might be an option; especially if a nice air-conditioned RV is part of the bargain. Whatever you enjoy as a means to unload, decompress, recharge your batteries, and get out of town is probably what your pastor enjoys. Don't be afraid to ask. The worst that can happen is that he or she might politely decline your invitation. However, they might say yes, which gives you an opportunity to care for your pastor in a fun way.

Have a happy and safe 4th!

*blah, blah, blah

Week of July 9 through 15

Defend him/her against critics

Can I just state here and now that sometimes ministry is tough. Pastors are the lightning rods for criticism in the church.

"The church **ought to**...."
"**Why doesn't** the pastor do....?"
"**Why did** the pastor do......?"
"In my last church **we did** things this way........"
"In my last church **we never did** things that way........."

The majority of problems people have with the pastor or the way the business of the church is conducted is because of differences of opinion. Did you catch that? *Differences of opinion*. Not sin. Not ethical or moral issues. Just different thoughts and opinions.

Gather 25 people together for a meeting and you'll get 25 different opinions. When someone dismisses, overlooks, or counters our opinion on an issue we tend to get our feelings hurt. *Come on, you know it's true!*

You have two choices in that instance: Get hurt or get over it.

I wish I could say that most people get over it. It has been my experience that they don't. Instead they talk about it. **A. Lot**. They will find someone who will listen to them and that person may pick up the gauntlet of offense and take it to another person. Depending on the situation a mini maelstrom can quickly develop.

The Bible is very clear about problem solving when differences come up between believers. Go *first* to that person and speak to them **before involving others** (Matt. 5:23, Matt. 18:15).

So *what are you to do* if you hear rumblings against your pastor or other leaders in the church?

Ask if they have spoken *directly* to the pastor (or other ministry leader involved) about the issue. If they haven't, then gently remind them of Matthew 5 and 18. Most people don't want to address/confront the pastor; they just want to complain to a listening audience.

Sometimes people need to be reminded that the pastor is just another human being who makes mistakes. Sometimes people need to be reminded that there are usually many ways to look at a particular situation and that their opinion is *just one* of those ways. Sometimes people need to be lovingly reminded that they are participating in gossip or hearsay. That may smart a bit, but it will be to their benefit.

Bottom line: Defend your pastor against criticism. Don't participate in idle chit chat or gossip. Encourage others to offer grace and mercy. Point them to Jesus. Challenge them to pray with an open heart and open mind. Your pastor(s) will be ever so grateful!

Week of July 16 through 22

Offer to babysit/take the kids overnight

Does your pastor have babies, young children, or even teens? Do you know if your pastor and his/her spouse have a regular date night? Have you ever thought about offering to babysit the kids or invite the kids to stay with your family overnight?

Obviously, you need to have a personal relationship with your pastor and his/her family in order to make such an offer. Otherwise, well………..stranger danger, and all that. But, if you do know your pastor and his/her family well, why not offer to watch the kids so the pastor and his/her spouse can have a night off? Depending on the kids' ages, you just may want to make it a sleepover. Why? (1) So your pastor and his/her spouse can have time to recharge their batteries. (2) So they can rekindle the flame that is threatening to blow out from a life full of nurturing other relationships to the detriment to their own.

Remember, this offer doesn't just extend to the guy up front. Think of the other ministry leaders in your church. Better yet, think of the spouses. Ministry can take its toll on a marriage. Giving your pastor and his/her spouse a chance to connect sans kids is a great blessing.

Don't just limit your offer to a date night though. Once kids enter the picture a ministry leader's spouse is often left out of ministry opportunities because of those little blessings. Is your church having a high school Bowl-A-Rama next month?

Do you think the high school pastor's spouse would be interested in chaperoning her husband and his 45 goofy charges for the night (yes, I meant to say chaperoning the high school pastor. Most HS pastors I know could use a chaperone)? If you offer to watch her *littles* she would be able to join in the fun.

So, come on all of you empty nesters, you'd love to refresh those diapering skills wouldn't you? Any singles out there? How about taking the tweens and teens out for the night to give the weary parents a well-deserved break? Your pastor and spouse (okay, probably mostly the spouse) will thank you!

Week of July 23 through 29

Volunteer in an area of constant need – one that he* mentions often

Do you know the areas of greatest need in your church? Quite often they are the ones your pastor or a ministry team leader mentions frequently from the pulpit or in the weekly bulletin. Is the nursery in need of workers? Is the parking lot a zoo between services? What about clean up after/between services?

One of the biggest headaches in church leadership is filling the constant need for volunteers. The church can only pay a limited number of people for their services and must rely on volunteers to fill in the gaps. There are fun jobs. Those get filled pretty quickly. Then there are the not-so-fun jobs. Those are the ones that seem to have a permanent place in the church bulletin **Help Needed** section. Have you ever given thought to volunteering for one of those?

"Yeah, but I don't do well with screaming babies."

"Yeah, but I can hardly manage to clean my own house properly each week. I don't have time to help keep the church clean!"

"Yeah, but it gets pretty hot in the summer and pretty cold in the winter. I don't like standing out in the elements directing traffic."

I'll bet we all can find some excuse rather than volunteering.

After all:

- Church is a place where you can leave your kids for an hour-and-a-half and let someone else care for them.
- Church is a place with sparkling floors and restrooms and a hygienic kitchen where you can grab that cup of coffee before service.
- Church is a place where bulletins are stuffed, prayer cards are send out weekly, and equipment is set up and torn down by happy church leprechauns, thus, leaving us free of any personal responsibility!!

Sadly, there are no real church leprechauns and the majority of the work is done by a very small minority (less than 20%) of the people; which includes the pastor, his wife, and his family members! Ask any PK (Pastor's Kid) about those dreaded 7:30 am phone calls from dad requesting that they get there early to clean toilets and empty trashcans because someone dropped the ball.

Good times......
So, if you want to care for your pastor. Volunteer............for the hard stuff! No one is looking for a lifelong commitment, but a few hours here and there go a long way in actually *showing* your pastor that you care.

*Tired of seeing this disclaimer? Me, too.

Week of July 30 through August 5

Loan him* your toys

We are now nearing the end of summer; at least summer according to the school calendar. In some parts of the country school children will be heading back to school in about two weeks, other areas still have several more weeks for fun in the sun.

According to most church calendars August is a slow month. VBS (Vacation Bible School) is long over. Youth group summer camp is a memory. Most families are home from their trips and are settling back into a routine.

Now that your pastor(s) have some time to breathe before ramping back up for Fall and all of the *Back to School* activities and Bible Study start-ups, would you consider loaning your pastor(s) some of your toys to enjoy before summer is officially over and the toys are put aside for the winter? Some of you may have personal water crafts such as Sea-Doos or Jet Skis, canoes or kayaks. You may have a boat that can tow a skier or a slow meandering pontoon boat. Perhaps you have a couple of dirt bikes or a dune buggy that is approved for off-roading. You know what kind of toys you have. Do you think your pastor and his/her family would enjoy a bit of fun? Do you own a sailboat? Why not offer the pastor's family a fun afternoon sail (with you as captain, of course)? Do you have camping equipment, an RV or fifth wheel? Pastors (most of them) enjoy camping just like you!

I have so many memories of church members generously offering my family a chance to get away for a day or two with some fun toys. One family owned a houseboat and would take us out for a few days to relax and ride their Sea-Doos. Another family would take us water skiing at a local lake from time to time. We've ridden horses, as well as motorcycles, on back roads courtesy of friends. People have been so incredibly generous sharing their toys with us over the years and we (our children included) have benefited in many ways. We felt loved. We felt appreciated. We felt honored. We felt included. We were able to relax and get away from every day stressors and laugh, play, enjoy each other and our friends.

Don't you want the same thing for your pastor(s)? If you have some toys and haven't yet made the offer to share them (go along if you're worried they might not be used correctly) then seriously consider doing so. There are only a few days left of summer. Be a blessing by blessing your pastor with some fun late summer memories.

*See disclaimer

Week of August 6 through 12

Provide a Sunday afternoon or a weeknight meal for the family

Have you ever been on the receiving end of a meal provided by another family or church member? During difficult times have people dropped by your house with dinner so you didn't have to trouble yourself to cook when you were recovering from surgery, a birth, or the death of a loved one? I have and it was wonderful.

Have you ever thought of providing your pastor's family with a meal for no other reason than **you were thinking about them and wanted to be a blessing**?

When I was a full time teacher, mother of three elementary school-aged kids, and a pastor's wife, a student's mom surprised me by bringing dinner for my family when she picked her child up from school. I can still remember how grateful I was and how honored I felt. There was no particular reason except that she'd been thinking of a practical way to bless me and thought providing dinner and dessert would do just that. It did. I remember how delighted I was to bring the food home (really good lasagna, if I remember correctly, salad, garlic bread, and a cake), heat it up, and then simply enjoy it. It is still a vivid memory because it only happened once - in 12 years of teaching.

Do you think you could do something similar for your pastor(s)? I'll bet you could call him/her up, text, email, or call the spouse and find out a good day during the week for you to drop something by their home or the church. A nice Sunday afternoon meal might be a great choice. I know that by the time Sunday rolled around I was tired of cooking, my husband was exhausted, and the kids just wanted to relax. If we didn't stop at a restaurant on the way home from church we usually just scrounged what was left over in the refrigerator. A home cooked meal would have been a real blessing.

Can't cook? No problem, that's what restaurant gift cards are for. The thought is the same either way. The intention is to be a blessing in a practical and, maybe, an unexpected way. This is especially practical if the family has allergies or dietary restrictions and the thought of cooking a gluten free or vegan menu is too daunting. In 30+ years of ministry I honestly can't think of a time that someone dropped off a meal "just because" and only once during 12 years of teaching. That's not to say we didn't have people care for us during times of hardship or need, we did. I'm referring to the *unexpected, out of the blue, no particularly special reason* meal drop off.

If it isn't practical for you to consider making a "just because" meal this week, then whip out your calendar and pick a future date(s) that would work for you. Coordinate this with your pastor (or his spouse, to be on the safe side) and begin planning a special meal. It doesn't have to be gourmet; chili and cornbread, homemade soup, taco meat with all the fixins' ---- you get the idea. It will be fun for you to plan and a blessing to your pastor's family; though do remember to ask about any dietary restrictions/allergies before you cook your pot o' blessing. Now, let your inner Julia Child loose!

Offer a professional service for a deep discount or for free

The long Dog Days of Summer are upon us. The weather is hot, the days are long, and the grass seems to grow a foot overnight. Do you have a landscape business? Would it be possible to swing by your pastor's house one afternoon and mow the yard and trim the bushes?

Many parts of the country experience frequent afternoon thunderstorms. Any car not parked in a garage would benefit from a good professional carwash and/or light detailing. If you own or work at a car wash you might consider a free wash.

Are you a dog walker or groomer? I'm sure your pastor's canine would benefit from your services. How about a dry cleaner, window washer, electrician, or plumber? You have something to offer your pastor as well.

What if you work in a profession that is associated with high fees such as an orthodontist, attorney, or podiatrist? You probably can't give away your services, but I don't think your ministry leaders would mind a discount.

Why would you want to do this? I'll give you a couple of reasons. I've mentioned previously that a pastor usually receives less income than another professional with a similar educational background. I personally don't know of any pastor that has gone into ministry for the money. Notice I said *personally*, we can all probably come up with a name or two of unscrupulous individuals. I'm not talking about *those guys*. Giving away a free or discounted service is a great blessing, especially to a family that may have a bit more month at the end of the money.

It is also a great way to get your name out there. It isn't self-serving to donate a free dental exam or oil change. Business people do it all the time. If you are an auto mechanic and do a good turn for your pastor, well then, you know he/she will do a good turn back by referring people to you. Nothin' wrong with that. In fact, you're helping your church community by giving them more options for honest, hard-working individuals when they, too, need your type of professional service.

So, what do you think? Is there some way that you can use your professional abilities to care for your church's ministry leaders in the near future?

August 20 through 26

Encourage ministry wives to seek out a mentor or fellowship with other ministry wives

This one is for all of the ministry wives out there. To all of you ladies that are married to men in pastoral and ministry leader positions, **thank you.** I appreciate you. I honor you. Why? Because I recognize that it isn't easy being married to a man in full-time ministry. Your life is unique. The challenges you face are unique. You may go from seasons of great highs where ministry is awesome and people are actually nice, to seasons of low-lows where you feel used, abused, and discarded. I know. I've been there.

Because your life and life experiences are unique I encourage you to seek out another ministry wife that is a bit further along in ministry than you are. Look for a woman who has some life experience and **can not only understand where you're coming from, but can give you some fresh perspective.** Ask God to bring a mentor into your life.

A mentor is simply someone who has experience and can be a trusted friend, confidant, and, if asked, an advisor. A mentor doesn't need a degree in counseling or a Ph.D. A mentor, in this case, is simply an older pastor's wife who has already navigated some of the challenges you are facing and has come through still walking in grace and mercy toward others. She is a woman who may have a few scars and bruises from life in ministry, but still loves Jesus, her husband, and the church.

When I was a younger woman I could have used a mentor in my life. I didn't know who I could turn to for counsel and advice. There were so many people that I couldn't look to for help and support; people in the church were out (I didn't want to harm my husband or our ministry during an unguarded moment), my friends couldn't relate, nor could my co-workers. I really could have used a mentor, but I didn't know where to find one and, quite honestly, I didn't give it much thought. I usually just marched along like a good little soldier and stuffed my feelings. Unfortunately, my husband was the target when the pressure had built up and I needed a place to vent. Fortunately, we weathered the storms and I've gained understanding about the need to have a trusted female confidant in my life.

If your church is part of a larger organization, find out if they have a fellowship specifically for ministry wives. Encourage your pastor's wife to seek out a mentor from that group or at least attend in order to have fellowship with her peers. Are you a seasoned ministry wife yourself? Will you pray and ask the Lord to lead you to a younger woman in order to reach out to her and offer her friendship and the benefit of your wisdom?

There are also some online sources. There are a couple of organizations that offer forums for pastors' wives to go online and talk to one another and encourage one another. A quick Google search should yield some results. I've recently started a closed **Facebook** group just for pastors' wives – *Standing Stone's Ministry Wives Rock*. It is in its infancy, but I hope that one day we have many women encouraging and praying for one another in a strictly confidential environment.

No matter the source, it is very important for ministry wives to have a safe and confidential way to vent and let off a little steam. A trusted mentor in her life is a very precious commodity. Therefore, if you are a ministry wife or know a ministry wife, I cannot urge you enough to seek out for yourself, or encourage your pastor's wife to seek out, a mentor or the fellowship of other ministry wives. No one should feel alone in ministry, not when there are resources out there.

Week of August 27 through September 2

Invite your pastor and his/her spouse to a gathering to meet your friends

This week's suggestion on one way to care for your pastor may be a bit tough for some people. The thought of inviting your pastor and his wife to a party with your friends might cause you to break out in a cold sweat. *"What? Introduce my pastor to my friends? Are you kidding me?"* Hold on for a second and let me explain why I think this is a good idea. (I won't even mention the fact that if you're hanging out with people you would be embarrassed to introduce to your pastor you might just be hanging out with the wrong people. That would condescending, wouldn't it? [Insert wink and Church Lady smile here]).

We live in a dark world - the tiniest bit of light shines brightly in a dark room. The tiniest bit of salt causes the whole glass of water to taste salty. As salt and light in the world Christians can greatly influence those around them simply by showing up and loving people. Not preaching. Not sermonizing. Not withdrawing. But by being gracious and showing kindness to others. Your pastor and his/her spouse can do that with your friends and family, perhaps in ways that you can't.

Some people view pastors as other worldly, not like *normal* people. Frankly that is probably because they haven't been around many pastors. When given a chance to get to know your pastor and your pastor's spouse, a friend or family member just might make a connection that could eventually lead to, *oh, I don't know*, your friend or family member's salvation perhaps?

My husband and I have been adopted by a very large family. We are invited to all of their family functions, even their family reunions. Because we've been frequently exposed to so many friends and family members we've been able to greatly influence several people, even leading many of them to the Lord. People who never attended church have sought out my husband when they needed advice, counsel, prayer, and premarital counseling. He has been involved with this family from birth to death and everything in between. He has baptized children and grandchildren in the ocean and in the family backyard pool. He's visited elderly parents in the hospital and officiated at weddings and funerals. When the family patriarch got sick my husband would regularly visit with him in his son's house and play cards with him (sorry to shock all of my Baptist friends!). This old curmudgeon, who didn't particularly like "preachers", looked forward to my husband's visits. He would be able to share his memories of days gone by while my husband listened. His heart softened toward the Lord over the course of these visits and just before he passed away his daughter-in-law was privileged to pray with him to receive Christ as Savior. She credits my husband with plowing the fallow ground and planting seed that she was able to harvest. What a joy and honor to be a part of such a family!

Now, your pastor might not become as involved in your family as the story above. That's okay. That's not really the purpose of this suggested way to care for your pastor. But he or she might! What is important is showing your pastor that **you care enough to invite him/her into your world**, even if it is just for an afternoon or evening. No one can predict where the Lord will take your relationship or what "coincidental" meetings (some call them divine appointments) your pastor may make while attending an event at your home. Don't be afraid to issue an invitation. Besides, your pastor (and wife) may just need to get out and laugh at a fun gathering that isn't church related. Have you ever considered that?

Week of September 3 through 9

Buy tickets for a movie, local sporting event, or concert

Now that summer is winding down our thoughts turn to college football (*Go Razorbacks!*), the start of professional football, or the upcoming World Series – *if you're a sports fan*, that is. New movies are opening every weekend through December 31st in order to be in the running for the Academy Awards. Concert venues that have been dark for the summer are ramping up before the holiday season. In short, there are lots of fun activities taking place right now and in the next few months.

Depending on your pastor's preference, why not invite him (or her) along to cheer the local college team? If you know she loves theatre, check out the upcoming offerings and order a couple of tickets. There are so many ways that you can bless your pastor (and spouse!) with tickets to an event. Fall is a great time to do it because there is a short window of time before holiday preparations take over and everyone is too busy to add one more outing to their calendar. Beat the holiday rush and make plans now.

When the Yankees played the Padres in the 1998 World Series my husband was the grateful recipient of an extra ticket; as a Yankees fan he had a blast (sorry Padres fans, it was pretty brutal). Similarly, a friend, who happens to be a more-than-rabid Seahawks fan, was given a trip to watch the Seahawks play the Broncos at the 2014 Super Bowl. He was ecstatic (before, and especially, after the game), to say the least.

While these are extreme examples, as I wouldn't expect anyone to feel obligated to buy World Series or Super Bowl tickets, you get the idea. Buying your pastor tickets to a game, show, or local art exhibit is a nice gesture, supposing your pastor actually likes any of those things. You'll have to do your homework.

Don't limit yourself to end of summer/early fall activities though. Find out what types of activities your pastor(s) enjoys and see if you can make something happen at a later date. Not all activities require spending money. There are often free concerts, movie nights, gallery openings, etc. Ask questions, then be creative. Make it a double date with the pastor and his/her spouse. Don't forget the kids! There are lots of fall activities that your families can do together.

As with most of these **52 Ways** I just want you to take the time to get to know your pastor on a deeper level by spending time with him/her doing activities that he/she really enjoys. If you belong to a mega church and know there is no chance of spending quality time with the lead/teaching pastor, don't worry about it. There are still tons of people at those mega churches in a pastoral/leadership position that you can get to know personally. It isn't just the guy up front that I encourage you to care for; I believe everyone in church leadership positions should be cared for in thoughtful ways. So, put on your thinking caps and let your creative juices flow.

Week of September 10 through 16

Write a letter of appreciation to your denominational headquarters or board members

Do you think your pastor is doing an awesome job? Do you appreciate the time it takes him/her to prepare the message every week, meet with church members, and take care of church business? Do you want to be an encouragement in his/her life?

Consider writing a letter of appreciation, not to the pastor, but to your denominational headquarters or church board members. I know, I know, letter writing takes time. It takes effort. In some cases it might take a bit of detective work to find an address or addresses. But the dividends are priceless.

In political circles emails are said to represent x number of people. Phone calls and faxes are given a higher number rating. Letters are given the highest rating. Why? Because it takes more effort to write or type a letter, address an envelope, and then actually mail the letter.

By writing a letter and mailing it to your denominational headquarters or to your church board members (in the event you are part of a nondenominational church) your actions are speaking very loudly. Your voice is heard very loudly.
Want to bet that your church's denominational headquarters or church board members receive negative communications

to a much greater degree than positive communications? It seems when people get riled up – in a bad way – they take the time to communicate their feelings. Yet, how many times have you been riled up – in a good way – and wanted to express yourself, but failed to do so?

Recently I had a great experience at a store. An employee went above and beyond to help me out. When I got home I called the store manager and expressed my appreciation. I felt really good about the gesture, the store manager was pleased, and ultimately the store employee was recognized for his outstanding service to the company. Is it okay to make the same effort to recognize the shepherds that go above and beyond to minister to me and my family? I think it is more than okay. It is an act of love.

Since snail mail isn't as popular as it once was I'm going to cut everyone some slack and suggest that sending an email is a perfectly acceptable means of communication. In fact, I encourage emails because those that spend a lot of time on their computers or phones won't have a hard time finding a denomination or church website and firing off an email or two. The sentiment and words are the same, no matter the means of communication.

This week would be a great week to send off a letter or email expressing your appreciation for your pastor(s). Do you agree?

Week of September 17 through 23

Set up a designated fund for your pastor(s) to use to take young men** out to coffee or meals in order to foster mentoring/discipleship relationships

This week I want to talk specifically to church board members or anyone directly involved in the financial decisions of the church.

The rest of you can read along, or go back over the previous weeks and see if there are any you missed.

Okay, ready? I'd like you to consider setting up a designated fund for your pastor(s) to use to foster mentoring/discipleship relationships. This doesn't have to be a huge amount of money, but enough to cover a daily coffee or weekly meal. You can set the budget and your pastor can work within those parameters.

Nearly every pastor I know – male and female – sets aside time weekly to meet with individuals in order to mentor/disciple them. It may be a quick breakfast before work, a lunch appointment, or a mid-afternoon coffee. Some days they may have all three! Unless your church has a coffee house/café on the premises with an open tab for the pastor, these meetings usually are paid out of the pastor's own pocket. When I headed up the women's ministry in a large suburban church I met almost daily with women outside of the church building, usually at my instigation, and usually I picked up the tab. Rightly or wrongly I considered it part of my tithe because the expense did add up at the end of the month.

I don't want anyone to have to choose finances over relationships. A mentoring or discipleship relationship is quite a bit different than a counseling relationship. When you are a mentor you meet regularly, you talk, you listen, you share, you encourage, you model, you instruct. You spend time together to build that relationship and a natural part of that seems to involve food or drink. My husband's "office" of choice is usually a local Starbucks or a nearby Corner Bakery. It just makes sense to meet at a public location that works for both parties, grab a bite to eat or a Frappuccino, and head to the big comfy chairs to talk for an hour.

Of course having a designated mentoring/discipleship fund isn't an absolute necessity, but it sure would be helpful. Just ask your pastor. By the way, I'm not suggesting you limit this fund to your lead or executive pastor only. Every area of pastoral ministry that involves people could and should involve mentoring relationships. Providing some funds toward fostering these relationships within the church will pay dividends far beyond coffee and sandwiches.

**Men mentor and disciple men. Women mentor and disciple women.

Schedule an appreciation Sunday

Don't you think it's lovely that people take the time to say nice things about the deceased during their funeral or memorial service? I've been at a few services with an open mic (not recommended) where it took a couple of hours for people to say all they wanted to say. I've often wondered, though, if those same people took the time while the deceased was alive to share those same sentiments. Probably not. We feel things in our hearts, but quite often those words are left unspoken. Which is sad. Why do we wait until the person is dead to say how much we loved and appreciated them?

I've always thought that it would be great if churches held a Pastor Appreciation Day every year or every couple of years to say all of the nice things that are on their hearts and minds, but never get shared out loud. Well, it turns out others have had the same idea and, lo and behold, there is an actual **Clergy Appreciation Day the second Sunday of October.**

So, rather than just thinking those nice thoughts, how about organizing your own Pastor Appreciation Day if your church doesn't currently schedule one? You can get all fancy or you can have a simple time of people sharing stories of how the pastor(s) of your church have touched their lives. You can have people write notes, send cards, or have a videographer film church members. Knock yourself out.

Our pastors are human beings. They have feelings that get hurt. They get tired. They get overwhelmed. They feel pain when they are misunderstood. They get discouraged when their efforts aren't always appreciated. **Just like you and me.** Scheduling a couple of hours once a year or every few years to honor and appreciate our pastor(s) doesn't seem like too much of a bother. Do you agree?

You can get a small group together to plan for a cake reception after Sunday evening service, a Pot O' Blessing after the church service, or whatever else strikes your fancy. Then pass the word to the congregation. Your pastor won't care if you plan a humble event (especially if it doesn't cost the church anything!), he will be overjoyed by your outpouring of love. She will be encouraged by your kind words.

Just like Mark Twain, I'll bet your pastor would say, *"I can live two months on a good compliment."* If that is the case, can you imagine how refreshing it would be to hear *many* good compliments? He/she will appreciate it. You will appreciate it. And, you might just get some great food or a tasty piece of cake out of the deal. Win-win, I'd say!

And, remember, it isn't just the guy up front that needs to be appreciated. There are so many areas of church leadership that seem to go unnoticed. Acknowledge and appreciate ALL those who serve in a pastoral role in your church.

Week of October 1 through 7

Invite them to your home for dinner

Want me to give you some insider information? Lean in close and I'll tell you……………………….your pastor's social calendar is not full for the next 10 years. While he/she may be very busy with church obligations there are probably very few scheduled dates that entail breaking bread with a member of the congregation around the family table. At least that was my experience.

When my husband and I pastored a smaller church we were occasionally asked into a church member's home for dinner. We always (well, usually) jumped at the chance to gather in the person's home to share food and fellowship. I promise you that I never judged a woman on her cooking skills, the beauty of her table, or the size of her home. We were just happy to spend time with people and to get to know them on a deeper level. We always left feeling loved and encouraged.

We've also been at some very large churches. During those years the dinner invitations to join a family in their home were few and far between. Dinners out at a restaurant were more frequent occasions, but not as many as one would think. When talking with other staff members we discovered the same thing. We came to the conclusion that people didn't issue invitations due to assumptions that we would be too busy to attend or that we wouldn't be interested in an invitation to join someone in their home. That's a pity because all of us, whether in a tiny church or in a mega church, are looking for connections with others.

The early church stayed busy visiting from house to house breaking bread together. That's how the church was built, it's in our DNA. Yet in our modern churches we seem to have forgotten the importance of fellowship over the dinner table. Sharing a meal, sharing stories, and sharing ourselves builds community. Who doesn't want to be a part of a community?

Do you hesitate to issue an invitation to your pastor for fear that you would be turned down? Then start off by making yourself known to your pastor. Make a point of speaking to him/her each week. Make a point to talk with the spouse. Show that you are interested in going deeper than a 3-second conversation while walking out the door. Do you have children? Issue an invitation to the Children's Pastor or the Youth Pastor. Don't be afraid to ask! Pastors aren't scary people. They like to eat just as much as the next guy, maybe even more!

I also want to encourage you to keep asking if you've been turned down a time or two due to other obligations. Sometimes a spur of the moment invitation works better than trying to schedule a time two, three, or four weeks down the road. Be flexible. Be spontaneous. Even the act of issuing an invitation is an encouraging thing. After all, that's the point of all of these 52 Ways - to be an encouragement to your pastor.

Week of October 8 through 14

Offer to mow the grass, run an errand, pick up a needed item

I have a book on my shelf that was given to my husband at a pastors' conference. The title is *Addicted to Busy*, by Brady Boyd. It has been sitting on the shelf gathering dust since my husband brought it home. Why? *Because we've been too busy to read it.* You saw that coming, didn't you?

All of us try to cram too much into every day. Pastors are no exception. In fact, they may be the poster children for *Addicted to Busy* (which was written for pastors, I think, since I haven't read it yet). Most pastors believe they are being productive when their schedules overflow with meetings and deadlines. What they don't realize is that over productive schedules day after day, year after year, lead to burnout.

One practical way you can help your pastor is by offering to take one of those items off of his/her **TO DO** (*OR ELSE*) list. If he doesn't hire gardeners to mow his yard, could you and your kids go over to his house on a Saturday morning and get the job done for him? Is there an event coming up at your church that you could lend a hand with? Most children's pastors are already making plans for Christmas and may need the help of a go-fer (someone who goes here and there picking up and dropping off items). It doesn't have to be church related; it can be a personal errand. Personal errands such has car repairs or trips to the hardware store take up lots of time and add stress to an already stressful day. If you're not overwhelmed yourself, you might just want to make a call and see if there is anything you can do to lighten the load.

My husband and I moved from the big city (big suburbia more accurately) to a more rural area of the country. Big city pastors and rural area pastors all have one thing in common – not enough time. In suburbia I can offer to take the pastor's car in for a smog check (required in California every two years) or get the tires rotated and the oil changed (which I can do while I shop at Costco). In rural America I can offer to pick up needed items at the hardware store or grab an extra bag of chicken feed while I'm in the town 45 miles away doing my weekly shopping. Location doesn't determine whether you can make an offer; it may just be a different kind of offer depending on your zip code.

So, here's another opportunity to put your thinking cap on and see if there is anything you can offer to do for your pastor(s), other church leaders, or the pastor's spouse in the way of giving a helping hand. If you do make the offer, don't be surprised if you get a blank stare or a startled look the first time you ask. Think about it, when was the last time someone offered *you* a helping hand for no other reason than to be a blessing? Mmmmhmmmmm.....thought so.

Week of October 15 through 21

Call his* wife and ask what kind of pizza they like. Order it, pay for it, and have it sent to your pastor's home

I really like this week's way to care for and bless your pastor and his family because it has to do with pizza. I really like pizza. It is a quick, easy, and practical way to show your pastor that you care. Even if your pastor or a family member is gluten intolerant there are gluten-free pizza options available out there.

But it really isn't just about pizza is it? It is about consideration. The gesture says "I've been thinking about you and your family and want to be a blessing in a small way." It is a small gesture in the grand scheme of things, but all of these types of small gestures add up in a big way.

It's all about the small things, folks.

It is easy to view the man up front each week as something super human. He is always upbeat and positive. He always has it together. His wife is always smiling and his kids are ~~always~~ usually well behaved and well dressed.

Um, not so much.

He gets cranky. Quite often he feels inadequate for the job at hand. He gets discouraged at times and some days he drags himself home from a rough day putting out lots of fires in the church. By the way, this isn't just true of the senior pastor. *All ministry leaders from every department have rough days.*

Now imagine, as he walks in the door of his home he smells the familiar aroma of his favorite Chicago-style deep dish pizza. He sees his favorite draft root beer sitting at his place at the table in a frosty mug. With a surprised voice he asks his wife if it is a special occasion.

"No. I got a call from the new family in church, you know, Frank and Becky with the three little girls? Well, Frank said he just wanted to bless your day and asked if he could order us our favorite pizza tonight. He paid for it and had it delivered right to our door! He even had them include a six pack of your favorite root beer! How thoughtful was that!"

Sounds fun, doesn't it? Fun for the recipient and fun for the one giving the pizza. Plus, it is an easy, practical way to say "I care."

*Yep, here's that disclaimer again!

Week of October 22 through 28

Send an encouraging note to his/her kids away at college

Most of the past *52 Ways To Care* have had to do with pastors, ministry leaders, and spouses, with a few directed toward the children. Today's post is about caring for his* adult children.

College is a transitional time in a young person's life. Some continue on in the belief systems that they brought with them from home, others can't shake off the ties from home fast enough. Either way it is a time of growing, learning, branching out, and discovering new things. It can also be a time of fear, self-doubt, confusion, and questions. It is a time when our young people are very vulnerable emotionally and spiritually. A letter from "home" or a card with an uplifting note is a reminder that they are loved and cared for. You don't have to know the pastor's son or daughter well in order to send a card. It really is *the thought that counts* when it comes to receiving mail.

Can you imagine how it will feel when your pastor's son or daughter receives cards randomly throughout the school year from family, friends, and even total strangers? He or she will be assured that the people back home are thinking about them and praying for them. They will know that they are loved.

If you have a relationship with your pastor's son or daughter that goes deeper than a quick hello while passing in the hallway you can go a bit deeper in your correspondence. You can ask if there are any specific prayer needs. You can offer to be a listening ear. You can offer to just "be there".

We never know how God will use us to minister into the life of someone else. Some meetings seem random and coincidental, others seem like divine appointments. God just might want to use you in the life of your pastor's child who is away at college. Sending cards and notes occasionally keeps that door of communication open. Or, your correspondence may just be a nice reminder of home and hearth. Either way it warms the heart.

One more thing; throwing in a $10 Starbucks gift card now and then wouldn't hurt either.

*Disclaimer

Week of October 29 through November 4

Upon hearing scandalous news withhold judgement and seek truth

Have you ever noticed how many television shows, newspapers, magazines, and websites report only outrageous and scandalous news? Do you ever wonder why there are so many of these types of publications? Because, in general, people loved to be shocked. We kind of love those jaw dropping moments when we can say, "Shut up! You've got to be kidding me!" Then we draw in a breath and our eyes just about pop out of our heads. I admit it, I've heard information and made instant judgements about the people involved without checking out the source. It's not something I'm proud of.

Have you been the victim of unseemly gossip or the main character in a story that is far from true? I have. It hurts doesn't it? It hurts deeply if people you love are repeating those stories.

Not all stories are gossip though. Sometimes people misinterpret what they've heard. We all have filters made up of past experiences through which we run information. Sometimes, when we take what we hear and run it through our filters we wind up with 2+2=5. But, **we may not know that our conclusions are faulty** if we don't ask further questions to gain clarity and understanding, or seek out the truth from other sources.

Case in point; recently two people were having a conversation about my husband. It went something like this:

Speaker **said**: *"I tell you, Ken bleeds Standing Stone Ministry."*

The intention was to tell the listener that if you cut Ken, he is so dedicated to the ministry of Standing Stone that *instead of blood* he would bleed Standing Stone.

Listener **heard**: *"Ken is bleeding Standing Stone."* (As in dry; using ministry funds and resources in a less than honorable way).

Fortunately this story had a happy ending where all parties involved discovered the truth of the misunderstanding, had a good laugh about it, and my husband's name wasn't tarnished.

Not all stories have a happy ending though. Someone can absolutely be an innocent party and yet, because false accusations were made or gossip or hearsay got out of control, and **even though the innocent person was exonerated**, the mud stuck.

Do you think the church is an exception when it comes to gossip, hearsay, and outrageous or scandalous talk? I wish I could give you a resounding "YES!", but that is not the case. Not by a long shot, which is so unfortunate I want to cry.

Here's the challenge. If you ever hear anyone say something about your pastor, a member of your pastoral staff, a pastor's spouse, or a pastor's child that makes your jaw drop and your eyes get wide, **STOP**. Withhold judgement. Ask questions to *gain clarity and understanding*. Find out how close the person sharing the information is to the source of the story (first person, secondhand, they heard it from the neighbor's plumber's cousin). Track down the truth or as close to the truth as you can get. And, most importantly, *refrain from sharing that information with anyone else, even if you believe it is true!* Instead, go to another pastor in your church, an elder, deacon, board member, or somebody in a position of leadership and share what you've learned **in confidence**. When brought to the attention of leadership they can track down and deal with a falsehood or they will be made aware of an existing problem that needs to be dealt with. Either way it minimizes gossip, brings health to the Body, and averts further damage.

Tell her you appreciate her and why

This one is for all of the pastor's wives out there who are, in my opinion, the unsung heroes of the church. Why do I say that? Well, quite often the pastor's wife is a BOGO or Two-fer. You know, you "buy" the pastor and get the wife and all that she does for free or "Two for the price of one." Not every church has a BOGO or Two-fer policy, but many do. It might not be explicitly verbalized, but in the minds and hearts of church members it is expected. Is the nursery worker too sick to come to church today? Call the pastor's wife, she'll sub. Would the ladies like to put on a Christmas Tea? I'm sure the pastor's wife would be happy to organize it or at least be a large part of the planning. Does the pastor's wife organize the potlucks, weddings, and Sunday school? In many churches across the US that is the case. She doesn't get a paycheck for it either.

Before I totally offend everyone let me say that most pastors' wives serve the church out of love for Christ and his Bride. She doesn't expect to get paid, even if the church could afford to pay her a salary. However, some do run ministries in the church and are compensated. In fact, I once served as interim Women's Ministry Leader for nearly a year, which was a paid position, and I surely appreciated that check each month! However, that was my only salaried job at a church in more than 30 years of ministry. I'm not complaining, I'm just stating facts.

The pastor's wife also shares her husband. She is often home with the children each evening while her husband is out ministering to others. She sits alone each week during the church service. She invites couples into her home in order for her husband to counsel with them. She is expected to smile at everyone and be gracious and kind, even though she may be hurting inside because some church members have been less than gracious and kind to her husband.

It's a tough gig at times. Other times it is the BEST. JOB. EVER!

Because you never know what is going on in the life of your pastor's wife – whether she is feeling loved and appreciated or frazzled and underappreciated – take a minute in the next week and tell her that you appreciate her and **why**. **Generalizations don't mean as much as specifics.** Be specific. And while you're at it, ask her if she has any specific prayer needs, then commit to praying for her. She will feel encouraged by your love.

Week of November 12 through 18

Love one another (and move toward health within your church)

"By this all men will know that you are my disciples if you have love for one another." John 13:35

Love. We talk about it. We sing about. We all need it. Why, then, is it so hard to show it at times?

When we have disagreements or when our feelings have been hurt by others we certainly don't feel their love and we may not feel very loving toward them. We experience this every day when dealing with family members, friends, neighbors, coworkers, or the guy driving in the lane next to us. We also experience this within the church because church is made up of family, friends, neighbors, coworkers and, yes, even the guy driving next to you.

Disagreements, even personality differences, between members of a church can cause real problems within the walls of the church and **quite often your pastor is caught in the middle**. Each party wants the pastor to *"do something"* to force the other party to apologize, concede, leave the church, or all three! Let me give you a few examples of real incidents that caused division, strife, and in some cases a church split:

- A young man broke off his engagement to a young woman in the church. Both sets of parents attended the church. The young woman's parents now hated the young man and a family feud ensued with friends taking sides essentially dividing the church in half; i.e., the Hatfields and McCoys, if you will.

- It was time to spruce up the sanctuary. One party wanted the same white color; the other wanted a pale blue. No one could reach an agreement. Eventually the church split. True story.

- The younger members of the church wanted to introduce more contemporary worship, while the more elderly members wanted to keep the worship songs and style exactly the same. The pastor's wife agreed with the younger members and made changes to add a mix of contemporary and traditional. Several older, more prosperous members, led by the organist and her husband, refused to tithe unless the traditional music service was restored. They hoped to force the hand of the pastor by creating a financial crisis.

While the above stories may be extreme, various scenarios such as these happen in churches every day. We allow our differences of **opinion and preferences** and our **current and past hurts** to dictate our actions and feelings. We forget to love. When we forget to love we forget to forgive. When we forget to forgive we tells others of the wrongs (sins) done to us. We then draw others into our disagreements and cause further division and strife within the body. Peter addressed this with the early church:

"Above all, love each other deeply, because love covers a multitude of sins." 1 Peter 4:8

Proverbs 10:12 puts it another way, *"Hatred stirs up conflict, but love covers over all wrongs."*

Let's face it. We've all experienced conflict with others. It is a part of our humanness to disagree; sometimes mildly, sometimes strongly. We have, and will continue to have, conflict in the church. Again, it is our human nature to want what we want, have strong opinions and preferences, and to feel hurt when we don't get what we want. Yet, we don't have to give in to our carnal nature and allow our feelings of hurt, anger, discontent, or any other emotion that can foster division between friends to rule us. We can choose love.

"Whoever would foster love covers over an offense, but whoever repeats the matter separates close friends." Proverbs 17:9

One of the best ways to care for your pastor and other church leadership is to love one another.

Commit to allow love to cover any present or former offense. Commit to keeping the matter between the immediate parties involved in order to promote healing rather than division within the church. Commit to being a disciple of Christ, known for your love for all men. Amen?

Amen!

Week of November 19 through 25

Find out from his* Administrative Assistant what books or periodicals he's been wanting for his library; order a few and have them sent directly to the church

It's beginning to look a lot like Christmas…..(cue Victorian carolers).

Yes, even though it is Thanksgiving and we're still finishing up leftover turkey, Christmas is in the air (and in the mall) and our thoughts turn to a nice gift for our pastor and other members of the pastoral staff. Soon the backroom counters will be overflowing with cookies, fudge, and assorted holiday sweets so now is the time to put on our creative thinking caps. Rather than packing up a few pounds of peanut brittle for your pastor (because by the end of the holidays he will be packing on a few pounds of his own!) try calling his Administrative Assistant and ask her (or him, but let's face it, most are women) what books or periodicals he's been wanting for his library; order a few and have them sent directly to the church. This works for other pastors on staff as well.

There is something great about holding an actual book in your hands, especially if it is an older book that you've searched the out of print archives to find.

When my husband was a new graduate from seminary he pined for a "Kittel", officially titled _Theological Dictionary of the New Testament_ – a 10-volume set written by Gerhard Kittel. It was very pricey at the time, as it still is actually. When the day came that he was finally able to purchase the set there was great rejoicing in the land. Over the course of more than three decades he used and appreciated his Kittel set quite often and with great satisfaction. My husband recently gifted that Kittel set to a young pastor he had mentored through Bible College. It was received with joy. Both the giver and the receiver felt blessed.

I'm sure there are books and periodicals that your own pastor would enjoy. Take a minute to find out and consider placing an order this week; just in time for a nice Christmas treat that will expand his mind _not_ his waistline.

*See disclaimer

November 26 through December 2

Pay for a gym membership............or not

Now that the holidays are officially upon us and most of us have been eating our way through the month of November, plan to eat all through December, *and* indulge ourselves on New Year's Eve, our thoughts will soon turn to New Year's resolutions or goals.

I'm not a fan of New Year's resolutions, but I am a fan of goals. I always make a list of goals for the New Year and quite often I itemize them by month. I love checking an item off the list as it is completed.

I've been overindulging a bit myself and the old yoga pants are feeling a bit tight in all the wrong places. I now have a goal to lose those pesky holiday pounds and to maybe *actually do* some yoga. I'll bet you're feeling the pinch too. The same goes for your pastor.

Wouldn't it be great to be able to help him/her get into shape while you help yourself as well? I don't like to go to the gym by myself, it is a bit intimidating in the free weight room when I'm alone, but I love to meet a friend or workout buddy there. I am more apt to actually go to the gym if someone is counting on me to show up. If you volunteer to be your pastor's workout buddy you'd be accomplishing two things at once. You would be compelled to exercise and so would your pastor.

Is a gym membership just too expensive for you to buy one for yourself and your pastor? How about asking several church members to go in on a membership with you? Perhaps one or two small groups would sponsor a membership for the pastor and his wife.

Is going to the gym not your thing? No problem. There are so many other ways to get some exercise and have some fun. One church I know has a small group that meets weekly for mountain biking. Another has a road bike group. I've personally been involved in a women's group that met every Saturday morning to run together. One year I asked a friend to train with me to walk a marathon. Perhaps your pastor or his wife would be interested in something like that.

Ever thought about issuing your pastor an exercise challenge? Recently I participated in a 1,000,000 steps in 100 days challenge. The goal was to average 10,000 steps a day. My secret weapon was my little electronic pedometer that synced with my computer to tracks my steps, my mileage, and my calories burned. There are many types of gadgets on the market that range from $10 to $100. Perhaps you could pick up one for yourself and one for your pastor or form a group and have everyone pitch in. Nothing like a little friendly competition between the pastor and his congregation!

Does this sound like fun to you? Pastors like to get out and exercise/play just as much as the next guy. You'll be doing your pastor, and perhaps his wife, a favor if you'll ask him/her to join you in some form of exercise. You'll build muscles and burn fat while building a relationship. What have you got to lose?

Week of December 3 through 9

Give the pastor's wife a gift card to a local grocery store or department store; this is especially welcome during the holidays

This week I'd like to continue the Christmas theme. There are always unexpected (as well as expected) expenses during the holiday season. The pastor's wife is quite familiar with this phenomenon. She is often expected to host a Christmas party for church staff. She is usually invited to various teas (many with $10 gift exchanges) and cookie exchanges. And, she may have invited lonely church members into her home for Christmas dinner (or she may be surprised when guests show up at the door that her husband invited but failed to mention – not that *I* have any personal experience with that!). To that end, grocery store gift cards are a double blessing during the holidays.

One year, when times were very lean, I was sad because our children would have very few gifts under the tree. My husband and I were never extravagant, but just opening the requisite new Christmas PJ's and packs of desperately needed socks and underwear would make for a bleak Christmas morning in our household. Lo and behold, a wonderful couple in our church pressed an envelope into my hand one Sunday morning about a week before Christmas. They decided to forego buying gifts for one another and instead gave the money to us to use toward our own

Christmas purchases. I was overwhelmed and humbled by the gift. God saw our need (yes, I know that our children were incredibly blessed already compared to 90% of the world's children, but *come on* – they're kids with childish reasoning, not mini adults) and used this amazing couple (who are still very much a part of our lives 20 years after the fact) to meet that need. I will never forget how grateful I felt to them and to our Heavenly Father.

So, yeah, grocery store, department store, Target, Walmart, and other store gift cards are a HUGE BLESSING to the pastor and his family during the holidays or *anytime* of the year.

Week of December 10 through 16

Tell him you appreciate him* and why

This is an easy way to care for your pastor and others. Simply tell him that you appreciate him and *why*. The *why* is important. We all love to be told specifically what we are doing right, don't we? Your pastor, as well as other leadership and staff members are no different. Giving a reason shows thoughtfulness and sincerity.

Check out the difference:
"Hey Pastor Jeff, I appreciate ya buddy!"

Um, okay, thank you.

Be more specific, like this:
"Hey Pastor Jeff, I really appreciate you! I love the fact that you make yourself available to everyone after the service and take the time to pray with people. Thank you!"

See? How easy was that? You don't need to lie in wait for your pastor after the service in order to share your *Top Ten List*. Just a quick word while you're going out the door is sufficient.

Don't stop at the pastor though. There are so many people involved in making church services run smoothly. Look around you. Do you see other pastors on staff? Don't be afraid to approach them, even if you don't remember their name at that moment, and speak words of appreciation. And please don't limit yourself to pastors only. Support staff and volunteers you see on a regular basis would appreciate hearing how much their service means to you.

So how about it? Do you think you could put this little tip into practice this weekend? It's easy, costs no money, yet pays eternal dividends. Don't underestimate the power of affirmation and appreciation and the difference your words could have in someone's life.

Do you appreciate your pastor? Do you appreciate your entire pastoral staff, leadership team, and various volunteers you see each week? Then, allow me to nudge you in the direction of sharing your thoughts.

Week of December 17 through 23

Take him* and his wife to a nice restaurant and *don't talk about church*

It's almost the end of our 52 ways to care for your pastor! If you've been with me from the beginning you'll have noticed that several of my suggestions to love, appreciate, and care for your pastor have to do with food. I've encouraged you to invite the pastor and his/her spouse out to lunch, call in a pizza order to be delivered to their home, and drop of a meal "just because". I've also mentioned inviting them to your home for a home cooked meal and I've even suggested that restaurant gift cards are a great option.

For my very last food fellowship-themed blessing may I suggest inviting your pastor and his wife out to a nice restaurant on a double date with you and your spouse? I'm not talking about Taco Tuesday here folks; I'm talking tablecloths and cloth napkins. Eating at a nice restaurant and getting a little dressed up is special – for everyone. Some pastors get invited to lots of lunch meetings or buffet-type gatherings, but having the chance to go out for the evening to a fancy(ish) place that doesn't involve a wedding reception, rehearsal dinner, or fund raiser is quite a treat.

Once everyone is seated, please refrain from talking about church issues. Instead, direct the conversation by asking your pastoral couple how they met and then sit back and allow them to tell their stories. Focus on the pastor's wife. She doesn't get a chance to talk about herself much. Give her the time to share her journey to faith, meeting her husband, becoming a mother...........whatever aspects of her life that she wants to share. I know you'll be tempted to jump in and share your stories. That's fine, once you've given your guests the chance to talk and talk and talk. Just remember, this evening is all about them and giving them a chance to share, **without interruption,** is a wonderful gift you can give to this precious couple. If they are hesitant to begin, just ask questions – not in an interrogational fashion, but with the heart to get to know them.

Make the evening very relaxed. Order an appetizer. Pass the bread and butter. Leisurely enjoy your entrée and if you have room, order dessert – even one for the table. Do whatever you have to do to make your ministry couple feel special, loved, and noticed.

Noticed? Was that a typo? No. I used the word noticed because of an experience my husband and I had with a sweet couple. He was the son of the founding pastor of their church. He grew up in the shadow of his gifted and beloved father. As the current senior pastor, he and his wife had spent more than a decade trying to live up to everyone's expectations to be just like his father and mother. By the time they arrive for a week-long marriage retreat with us they were tired, ready to burn out, and feeling defeated. The first morning of our retreat we asked him to share his story. He talked all through breakfast. He talked all morning. He talked through lunch. After an afternoon of rest, he talked before dinner, through dinner, and into dessert. He talked until it was time for bed. The next morning he thanked us for listening and said he felt a little sheepish for dominating the conversation the previous day, but then he said this, "In my entire life I have never been given the opportunity to tell my story in chronological order from birth to the present day. No one has ever cared enough to really listen to what I had to say. No one asked questions." At the end of the retreat the phrase that came to them was **ICU**. Their retreat week was like an **Intensive Care Unit** for them as individuals and as a couple. But, it also was a time that they felt noticed. They felt like we saw them – warts and all (and still accepted them). They felt like God had refreshed their hearts with the knowledge that *He also saw them*. ICU/**I See You**. They no longer felt invisible.

Your pastor(s) need to be noticed; for who THEY are, not just WHAT they do. So do their spouses. An invitation to a special restaurant and a chance to be heard is a powerful way to care for your pastor.

*See disclaimer – for the very last time!!!

Week of December 24 through 31

Commit to regularly pray for your pastor throughout the next year

This is it! The last week of our 52 Ways...... or, is it just the beginning? I've given you many, many suggested ways to show your pastor, pastoral team, church leaders, spouses, and PK's that you care for them. Now the ball is in your court. Have you done any of the previous 51 ways? Do you plan on doing any of them in the future?

For this last week I'd like to suggest, *again,* that you make a commitment to pray for your pastor on a regular basis. Prayer is such an important job for everyone in the church. Everyone. It is so important, in fact, that I'm going to reiterate our very first suggested way to care for your pastor from one year ago. I'm not only going to ask that you make a personal commitment to pray, but that you make a formal commitment by forming a group that regularly meets to pray specifically for your pastors, their spouses, and their children.

I think we fear joining a prayer group because we are convinced it will take too much of our time. We get it in our heads that if we aren't spending an hour praying it doesn't count for much. However, that simply isn't the case. Yes, you could form a weekly one-hour prayer group, but you don't have to in order to be effective. You could grab a couple of friends and meet 10 minutes before church service. You could devote the first five minutes of your weekly Bible study group or small group to pray for your pastor. The time involved doesn't matter, prayer matters. So simply pray!

I'm going to go even further and get a little crazy on you and suggest that you fast now and then and use that time to pray for your pastor. By fast, I mean giving up something you would normally eat or drink. For instance, you could do a dedicated fast and spend part of your fast praying for your pastor and your church (and the church at large) in your prayers. Some churches do a yearly month-long fast to begin the New Year. But, fasting doesn't have to mean giving up all food and living on water. You could fast a day, a couple of meals, or just part of a meal. I could decide to forgo my afternoon snack of milk and cookies and instead use that time to pray for my pastor. That is considered a fast because I've given up something and dedicated the time I would be eating to prayer. Easy, right? Do you think it is a possibility that you could incorporate some form of a fast in your time of praying for your pastor? You don't have to though, but you certainly can.

The bottom line is to become a people of prayer. Prayer should be our first resort, not our last. So, when you pray for your pastor let me give you the same list I gave you on week #1.

Pray for wisdom.
Pray for God's peace on him and his family.
Pray for strength.
Pray for encouragement.
Pray for health.
Pray for inspiration.

Pray for a closer walk and for time to spend on his own in prayer and the word. You'd be surprised at how many pastors struggle with their own personal devotions.

It's worth repeating that Satan doesn't want us to pray for our pastors, or anyone else for that matter, so expect some resistance. Expect to fall asleep quickly if you intend to pray the last thing at night before sleep. Expect the phone to ring the second you begin. Be prepared to push through the distractions and then.........simply pray!

There you have it! Number 52 of *52 Ways to Care for Your Pastor*.

My hope and prayer is that you have been blessed as you have been a blessing to those who love you and care for you on a regular basis. It is also my hope and prayer that this book doesn't wind up on the shelf to gather dust for several years. I'd love for you to begin all over again and try to do some of the suggestions next year that you missed this year, or, do some of the same ones again, especially those that you and your pastor(s) enjoyed the most.

Still reading? Stop right now and pray. Then put this book next to your new calendar and fill that puppy up with fun ways to show you care.

I'd also LOVE to hear from you. If you have any comments or suggestions please feel free to contact me at Leslie.e@standingstoneministry.org. I'd also love to hear your stories. When these 52 Ways first ran as a weekly email/blog post I heard from lots of people who shared great

stories. If you are a pastor and have benefited from some of these suggestions I'd love to hear from you too!!

May God bless you and continue to fill your heart with His love and may you take that love to others. This world definitely needs more love!

Shalom.

Made in the USA
Coppell, TX
19 November 2019